Tandava
In Quest of Shiva

Tandava
In Quest of Shiva

Tandava

In Quest of Shiva

Mukunda Rao

**MOTILAL BANARSIDASS
INTERNATIONAL
DELHI**

First Edition : Delhi, 2025

© Author
All Rights Reserved

ISBN : 978-93-48911-41-4

Also available at :
MOTILAL BANARSIDASS INTERNATIONAL
41 U.A. Bungalow Road, (Back Lane) Jawahar Nagar, Delhi-110007
4261/3 (Basement), Ansari Road, Darya Ganj, New Delhi-110002
Shop#. 6, 241, Luz Ginza Complex, Luz Corner, Mylapore, Chennai - 600004
12/1A, 2nd Floor, Bankim Chatterjee Street, Kolkata - 700073

Stockist : Motilal Books, Ashok Rajpath, Near Kali Mandir, Patna-800004

No part of this book may be reproduced in any form or by any electronic or mechanical means including information storage and retrieval systems without permission in writing from the publishers, except by a reviewer who may quote brief passages in a review.

Printed in India by
MOTILAL BANARSIDASS INTERNATIONAL

Other Books by the Author

Fiction
- *Confessions of a Sanyasi* (1988)
- *The Mahatma: A Novel* (1992)
- *The Death of an Activist* (1997)
- *Chinnamani's World* (2003, 2024)
- *Shambuka Rama: Three Tales Retold* (2018)

Non-fiction
- *The Other Side of Belief: Interpreting U.G. Krishnamurti* (2005)
- *The Penguin U.G. Krishnamurti Reader* (Ed.) (2007)
- *The Biology of Enlightenment: Unpublished Early Conversation with U.G. Krishnamurti* (Ed.) (2011)
- *Between the Serpent and the Rope: Ashrams, Traditions, Avatars, Sages and Con Artists* (2014)
- *The Buddha: An Alternative Narrative of His Life and Teaching* (2017)
- *Sky-clad: The Extraordinary Life and Times of Akka Mahadevi* (2018)
- *Belief and Beyond: Adventures in Consciousness from the Upanishads to Modern Times* (2019)
- *India's Greatest Minds: Spiritual Masters, Philosophers, Reformers* (2022)
- *The Indian Book of Big Ideas* (2023)
- *Babasaheb Ambedkar: An Inspirational Life* (2025)
- *I Think, Therefore I Ask: A Handbook for Intelligent Living* (2025)

Content

1. Om Namah-Shivaya — 1
2. Mahadevi — 7
3. Devara Dasimayya — 19
4. Prabhudeva — 26
5. Allama — 41
6. Married to God — 57
7. Anna Basava — 75
8. Allama meets Muktayi and Siddarama — 106
9. A Nameless Thief and Gowravva — 119
10. Somavva — 130
11. Bahurupi's Dilemma — 141
12. Kalyana — 148
13. The Throne of Void — 154
14. Challenging Allama — 163
15. Mahadevi's Trial — 174
16. To Kadali — 185
17. Basava's Trial — 192
18. Massacre in Kalyana — 203
19. Om — 209

Afterword — 223
Glossary — 225

Om Namah-Shivaya

It was the night of the new moon during the dark half of the month of Magha. On the banks of river Cauveri, the Shiva temple rumbled with continual ringing of bells. Outside the temple, the flares of burning torches atop four corner-poles lit up the stage and, like incensed serpents, hissed and danced furiously to the gusty winds. The chants of *Om namah-shivaya...* rose to a crescendo.

It was the Night of Lord Shiva.

Bahurupi Chowdayya, clad in a long ochre robe and an orange turban, appeared on stage like an apparition from the world of spirits. As the chanting crowd fell silent like a spent force, his eyes gleaming white, Bahurupi moved to the edge of the stage and thundered:

'Everything is a story within a story, like a circle within a circle. There are only stories, yours, mine and of the Great Unknown that is everywhere and in everything like salt in the sea.'

Bahurupi, the one with many faces, is a teller of stories, and such fascinating stories on hearing which even the gods are believed to rock with joy and wonder. And this Bahurupi, with plump cheeks and smiling lips and bright eyes, becoming an illustrious storyteller is in itself a strange story. Dire necessity and sheer practical sense had driven him into storytelling. For years he had lived the life of a charvaka, a hard-core materialist, who believed that if you didn't have oil at home, borrow ghee from the neighbour; the present is all, for who knows if there will be a tomorrow, especially for the neighbour. Ensconced in the comfort of this philosophy, our Bahurupi borrowed money recklessly and fell into heavy debts. And every time a furious money lender came to his house, Bahurupi would tell him such convincing stories and put up such a touching performance that the money lender, overwhelmed with guilt, would apologise profusely and leave.

One night, however, poor Bahurupi ran out of luck. Just as he was trying to sneak into his house through the backyard, the money lenders, who had been waiting for him in the dark, pounced upon him and beat him badly. Paru, his wife, who was fair and slim and beautiful and a head taller than him, rushed out in panic, but did not intervene. After the money lenders left, cursing and threatening to finish him off if he didn't return their money, she only said, 'Good-for-nothing rascal, liar, cheat, loafer, if you can't do any useful work, why don't you at least put to use this crooked ability of yours to earn some money.'

It was of course no crooked ability; if it were then we would call all our great storytellers crooked and dishonest. But then, Paru had a point, and Bahurupi, though terribly hurt, had to concede. And to prove himself to his wife, our Bahurupi, a consummate liar, a con artist, became a storyteller.

Behind Bahurupi came Nageya Marithande, the laughing one, carrying a tabor drum and a long stick. The drum was meant to awaken people from both stupor and too much excitement, and the stick to drive away the illusion of knowledge. Clad in a loose gown, with thick-black curly hair that fell about his shoulders, sharp nose, thin lips and large kohl-lined eyes, and a perpetual laughter in his mouth, the clean-shaven Nage looked quite effeminate. But when he spoke it was in the booming voice of a man, which drove the crowd hysterical with laughter.

Now, as the temple bells thundered yet again, the wind shrieked and the flares crackled, he beat the drum three times, waved the stick three times and, planting himself by the side of Bahurupi, he said, 'My dear brother, why do you confuse people? Look at them eagerly waiting for your story. Come on now, give them a story.'

'Isn't everything a story, my friend?'

Nage beat his drum again, paused significantly, winking and smiling roguishly at the crowd. Then, suddenly, he shrieked, 'Yes, everything is a story; rather, a glorified gossip. Gossip turned into an art and trade. Come on now, out with your story.'

While some sniggered, many burst out laughing. Not everyone liked Nage, especially the saranas who were quite touchy about their faith, for they found many of his jokes quite wicked and blasphemous. He joked about everything, making no distinction between the sacred and profane; and made fun of everyone, whether god or human. Even so his jokes were legendary. It is said that on hearing his jokes, the usually grim-faced and terribly serious Jains, the charming yet deceptive Hindus, the generally solemn and humourless Buddhists, and even the subversive, skull-bearing Kaapalikas, loosened up, laughed themselves silly, forgetting their gods and goals. And the legend has it that once, even Lord Shiva couldn't help himself burst out laughing at his jokes.

Now Bahurupi raised his hand to silence the laughing and sniggering ones. 'Listen, and listen carefully,' he bellowed. 'This is no ordinary story. This is the story of the dead man walking. This is the story of the toad that lapped up the sky, of the snake that swallowed the snake charmer, of the child born of a barren woman. The story of maya who painted herself with colours of the rainbow, and the story of void that fell into void and grew up in void to sing without words, without sound, the song of life with no beginning and no end.'

'Om namah-shivaya,' chanted Bahurupi, 'Om namah-shivaya,' chanted the crowd after him. Then Bahurupi put his palms together, bowed in greeting and obeisance to humans and gods, to spirits and elements of the universe. 'Om...' he chanted yet again and then started on his now famous prelude to his story.

'Brothers and sisters, listen closely. All roads lead to Kalyana, where the story begins and ends, but mercifully, rather playfully, or, tragically, if you prefer, leave behind its traces for yet another beginning. Kalyana is the city of seekers from the beginning of time, and of their gods who now hide in free verses. You'll meet there the compassionate Basava, the architect of Kalyana, and his militant followers. You'll meet Mahadevi Akka, the ultimate devotee; and, the guru of gurus, the awe-inspiring Allama.

'All spiritual journeys, all stories end at Kalyana. There you finish yourself, and, sky-clad, move on to Kadali, the forest untouched by human civilization. There, in the primeval forest, you are no more. For, at Kadali, there is no fear or desire, no pleasure or pain, and no yearning for things that do not exist.

'Alone, Shiva wanders the forest of Kadali, his hair matted in ascetic locks, his mind burning with a single thought: *annihilation*. Friends, you know that without annihilation there is no creation. Creation and destruction, like life and death, are a simultaneous process, the very movement of life. And that, my dear fellow travellers, is *bayalu*, Open Space, Void; that is, *arivu*, Awareness that has no beginning, middle or end.

'That iss, *sat*, existence!

'Shiva is *sat*, existence. He is also *chit* and *ananda*, consciousness and bliss. The last one is the invention of the middle. The middle is the mischief, the play, the maya. And Shiva is both: the player and the play.

'Ah! You cannot think beyond Shiva! You cannot improve upon Shiva, for you cannot improve upon zero. But when you add a number to the zero, Shiva springs into being. Shiva is both being and non-being. Shiva as being embodies all human sentiments and all the qualities and properties of the universe.

'Shiva is all things.

'Friends, the idea of beginning is an illusion, since every beginning is already a second one, a third one, a hundreth one. It's a terrific cycle, never ending.

'And now listen closely. Once, at the end of a kalpa, an aeon, in the waters of the great deluge, Lord Vishnu was immersed in his yoganidra, when there appeared before him, Lord Brahma. Awakened by Brahma's presence, Vishnu opened his eyes and saw him smiling.

"Who are you?" asked Vishnu.

"Don't you know me? I am the Creator of the Universe," said Brahma.

"How can that be?" challenged Vishnu. "I am the Originator of the Universe."

'A fierce argument ensued between the two gods, each claiming to be the real maker of the universe, when there appeared before them a huge lingam of fire, with tongues of flames blazing out of it.

"Ah, what is this?" wondered Vishnu, and then turning to Brahma, he asked, "If you created everything, then who created this pillar of light?"

'Brahma had no answer, nor Vishnu. So, curious to trace the origins of this column of fire, Brahma assumed the form of a swan and flew skywards, while Vishnu took the form of a boar and burrowed down into the earth. Thousands of years passed, but neither of them could reach either the top or the bottom of the pillar of light. Exhausted, they returned to the surface of the earth, and meekly, agreed that there indeed existed a God who was greater than both of them, and surrendered themselves to the pillar of light with humble prayers. Shiva then appeared out of this column of fiery lingam, with a thousand arms and legs, with the sun, moon and fire as his three eyes.

"We are born of the same source," said Shiva, an intriguing smile creasing his deep-blue lips. "We are now complete. We are one," he declared, banging upon his drum and starting to dance. And, as Vishnu and Brahma joined him in, Shiva bellowed: "Let the play begin."

Mahadevi

Omkara Shetty stood outside the threshold of his two-storied house, fuming and fidgeting. He was a stout, balding man in his early forties. It was getting dark and Mahadevi was not yet home. From tomorrow he should stop her from stepping out of the house, he decided. He should not have let her remain unmarried for so long. Girls at her age were already married with children. She might be quite different from other girls, but she was a girl after all.

Shaking his thinning hair, Shetty went inside to find his wife, Lingamma, in the kitchen, preparing to cook the evening meal. As she turned to face him, the evening yellow light crept through the lone window and lit up her expectant face. With a heavy heart, Shetty asked, 'Have we done something wrong?'

'What can I say?' murmured the wife. 'You know her.' She was a short woman with long, curly hair and a pleasant, smiling face, and looked several years younger than Shetty.

'I really don't know,' cried Shetty in sudden despair. 'Sometimes I wonder if she is really our daughter. I don't see a single trait either of you or me in her.'

'She has my curly hair,' said Lingamma, an impish smile escaping her lips. 'But I think she takes after my grandmother.'

He felt a sudden surge of anger, but checked himself, feeling somewhat lost and then began wondering if he really understood anything at all, least of all his wife and daughter. How could she say that Mahadevi resembled her grandmother who had been such a disgrace to the family? Three months after the death of her husband, didn't the shameless woman run away with a musician, leaving behind her only son to be brought up by her in-laws?

Shetty scowled. He was in no mood for an argument, certainly not standing in the kitchen where his wife rigned supreme and made him feel like an intruder. 'I think I'll go and fetch Mahadevi,' he said, growing edgy.

'But why are you so tensed up?' asked Lingamma, frowning, as she followed him into the hall.

And there she was, at the door, her long and luxuriant hair framing her beautiful oval face and large, intelligent eyes, like a goddess materialised from the heavens. And behind her stood Chennayya, the middle-aged associate of Guru Lingadeva. He bowed to the couple with joined hands and then left like a man in a hurry.

Mahadevi was smiling, her face aglow with some new-found joy. 'Appa,' she announced excitedly, 'I composed two vachanas today. You want to hear them?'

His annoyance gone, wide-eyed, drinking in the strange beauty of his daughter, Omkara Shetty stood as if in a trance, and behind him hung Lingamma, smiling knowingly.

> *You freed me*
> *from the clutches of ignorance,*
> *from the web of samsara.*
> *You opened my eyes to*
> *Lord Chennamalikarjuna.*
> *I am blessed,*
> *Guru Lingadeva.*
> *I have found my destiny.*

Breathless, she continued with her second composition.

> *The sun is the seed*
> *for the worldly mischief,*
> *the mind is the seed*
> *for the human mischief.*

> *My mind rested in You,*
> *O Lord Chennamalikarjuna,*
> *I have no desire, nor fear;*
> *this worldly life is not for me.*

Tears veiled Omakara Shetty's eyes and he didn't know what to say, or even what to think. It seemed as if he was looking at his daughter for the first time. Studying her, he marvelled at her long curly hair that seemed like aerial roots of a great banyan tree, flowing down her body like waterfall. Clad in a sari she looked a pretty young woman. Her light-brown skin shone like gold, her arms were as fine as lotus stalks, her waist slender and womanly, and her breasts strained against the tight blouse. She was quite tall, taller than her mother, almost his height. She wore no jewels except for the tiny gold earrings, but her forehead was smeared with holy ash. Shetty frowned, feeling somewhat embarrassed.

Three years ago, when Guru Lingadeva suggested that they send Mahadevi to the matha, so that she could learn the scriptures, Shetty had readily consented. 'She is quite sharp and intelligent beyond her age,' the guru had said. 'You know best,' Shetty had replied and had thought that his daughter's going to the monastery could do nothing but good to her. At first, Mahadevi only attended the scriptural classes in the morning hours and returned home before lunch. But, as days passed, she began to spend almost the whole day at the matha and came home only in the evening, but well before her father would return from his work.

One day, when Lingamma scolded her for coming home late, Mahadevi had said, 'What will I do at home? There is so much to learn at the matha.'

Screwing up her eyes, more in mock anger than real frustration, Lingamma had asked, 'But when will you learn household work and cooking? What will I tell your father?' Since then, Lingamma had started grumbling and scolding her for not helping her in the household chores.

Getting irritated, Mahadevi would snap, 'Stop whinging. I'll never learn household work and cooking.'

'If you don't learn now, what will you do in your husband's home tomorrow? Will your Chennamalikarjuna come and do the household chores?'

'Chennamalikarjuna will be my husband and he'll not let me do any such work,' Mahadevi had replied, with an impish smile just like her mother's.

Mahadevi was their only child, born almost six years after their marriage. 'Do not despair,' the guru had said when the unhappy couple had sought his advice, 'and do not lose faith in Shiva.'

When the girl child was born, Omkara Shetty was disappointed, but he did not show it. A son would follow soon, he hoped, but it never happened. And he began to devote more time to his business, leaving the task of bringing up the child to his wife, and Guru Lingadeva, who had become more of a doting father to Mahadevi than a family guru. He came home almost every other day and spent long hours playing with the child. His fondness for Mahadevi intrigued many in the neighbourhood. Omkara Shetty too found the guru's attachment to the child very strange, something that did not go well with his spiritual vocation. And during the days he was at home, it hurt and angered him to see little Mahadevi, ignoring him, rush towards the guru as soon as he had stepped into the house.

She was no more his little girl now; she had grown and changed much beyond his imagination. All her girlish qualities had evaporated in the heat of her new-found devotion to the learning of the scriptures and to her Lord Chennamalikarjuna.

'Look at her! Is she the little girl I used to know?' Shetty wondered.

'So what do you think?' asked Mahadevi, now looking expectantly at her father. Then noticing the tears in his eyes, feeling somewhat awkward and nervous, she asked, "Father, have I done something wrong?'

'No, no,' Shetty said, wiping the tears with the back of his hand. 'I—I, don't know,' he said, 'you have changed...you have become a poet!'

'I'm not a poet,' said Mahadevi, giggling with relief. 'And this is not poetry, father.'

That night, unable to sleep, Shetty kept tossing and turning in his bed. Being a devotee of Shiva, he should have been happy, he tried to tell himself, but instead he only felt troubled by self-doubt and fear. Turning to his wife, who seemed least disturbed and already fast asleep, he spoke heavily to her back, 'We should have got her married. We did a mistake. She is old enough to be a mother of two.'

Lingamma was awake. She turned on her side and stared, not without concern, at her husband's distressed face in the faint light of the lamp kept in the niche of the wall.

She asked, 'Don't you remember what she says in her vachana?'

Shetty shook his head, wondering what Mahadevi's vachana had got to do with what he was saying.

'"This worldly life is not for me..." that's what she says,' Lingamma said.

Shetty did not care to remember and he did not think a young girl's playful composition had to be taken so seriously. But he asked, 'What do you think?'

'I don't know.' Lingamma sighed. 'She doesn't look like she'll marry at all.'

'What are you saying?' Shetty almost shouted. 'You want her to become a sanyasi?'

'If that's the will of Shiva, who can prevent it? Now go to sleep,' she snapped and turned her back to him, muttering to herself, 'I knew, I knew it would all come to something like this.'

'You have to climb five hills and transcend the five senses to reach the heart of Srishaila, where Lord Chennamalikarjuna resides. Between two hills, deep in the valley, lives our Lord. Some distance away from the temple, flows river Krishna. Behind the temple, from the underground, springs the sacred Ganga, where you wash yourself clean of all impurities, go round the temple and come upon the Jyothirlinga, the Lord of Light. It is of course an arduous journey, but with the name of the Lord on your lips, you never feel tired. It takes about ten days and by the time you arrive at the valley, your entire past would have been dissolved. But still, it is not the final destination, nor does it bring about the final dissolution of your self. After you meet with the Lord, pray and commune with Him, you have to move on, climb two more hills and then bypass the vast plantain grove to enter deep into Kadali. Without the help and guidance of the chunchuru tribe there, you would be lost. Not many go there. In fact, in the last twenty years, no one there has either heard or seen anybody going into the forest. Deep inside, there are huge rock caves where many of our sages are believed to have meditated and come upon the truth. Of course, I did not even think of going there. It's beyond me, you see,' said the jangama, smiling wryly.

The wandering monk was short and his skin the colour of the bark of a pipal tree. He was naked except for the narrow piece of cloth over his groin held up by a string around his waist. His long hair and shaggy beard framed a surprisingly youthful face. It was difficult to assess his age. But from the stories he narrated one could imagine he was at least fifty years old.

'I'm not ready, not yet, you see,' confessed the monk, with a disarming smile. 'But then, it doesn't depend upon your courage or will, you see; rather, it is the cessation of the will that does the trick. You should be ready to drop dead. But you cannot consciously drop dead, can you?'

Guru Lingadeva smiled knowingly. 'You must be tired,' he said to the jangama. 'Why don't you please eat something and rest for a while.'

The jangama laughed as if it was a joke. 'But I have already eaten,' he said, 'and I'm not tired.'

'You ate just two bananas,' protested Lingadeva. There were still a few more ripe bananas and an assortment of dry fruits left on the plate kept in front of the jangama.

'Two full bananas and a jugful of water, isn't that enough for this little body?' guffawed the jangama.

Mahadevi sat among the devotees, listening to the jangama's story with rapt attention. She told herself, 'Chennamalikarjuna is my Lord. Kadali is my destination.' And then suddenly, as if driven by some inner force, she sprang to her feet, went over to the jangama and kneeling down in front of him, touched his feet with reverence.

Jangamas never touched the body of a woman, nor allowed women to touch them, even if it was meant to seek their blessing. Loud sighs and little grunts of disapproval broke from the crowd. The jangama smiled as if amused. Looking into her eyes, he asked cryptically, 'What are you doing here, mother?'

In the evening, there was a congregation of the devotees from Uduthadi. Lingamma was there among the few women who all sat on one side, a little distance away from the men folk. Facing the bhaktas sat Guru Lingadeva and by his side, the jangama. The bhaktas had come to have darshan of the jangama and listen to his discourse. But the jangama didn't seem too enthusiastic to speak, or he thought he had spoken enough. 'Chant some vachanas,' he muttered and shut his eyes. The chanting of vachanas by the young novices began promptly. At one point, Lingadeva looked at Mahadevi and signalled her to sing. And Mahadevi sang one of Basavanna's vachanas that was her favourite.

> *Cripple me father,*
> *so that I may not go here and there.*
> *Blind me father,*
> *so that I may not look at this and that.*
> *Deafen me, father,*
> *so that I may not hear anything else...*

A strange silence enveloped the gathering. For the first time in the matha they were listening to a girl chanting Basavanna's vachana. It came as a surprise even to Lingamma. She had not heard her daughter chant before and she had such a mellifluous voice! Her heart swelling with pride, Lingamma wiped her happy tears with the pallu of her sari. There were murmurs of displeasure, also appreciation, and then someone from the back row remarked, 'Look, there's already such an ascetic glow on her face and she's only a little girl...' A thin smile playing on his lips, the jangama kept rocking backward and forward on his folded, spindly legs. Guru Lingadeva smiled, willing his favourite disciple to go on.

And Mahadevi continued:

> *Listen, sister, listen, brother,*
> *I had a dream.*
> *I saw rice, betel, palm leaf*
> *and coconut.*
> *I saw an ascetic*

> *come to beg.*
> *I followed on his heels*
> *and held his hand,*
> *He who goes breaking*
> *all bounds and beyond...*

The jangama's eyes flew wide open and he shouted, 'I have not heard this one before, whose vachana is this?'

A slight shiver ran up Mahadevi's spine. She glanced at her Guru with a sense of foreboding. Lingadeva smiled, and whispered to the jangama, 'This is Mahadevi's own composition.' And he pointed out the long-haired Mahadevi, sitting among the students.

'Oh,' said the jangama and started to laugh. His loud laughter seemed somewhat inappropriate in an otherwise profound ambience. Before long he quietened down and bellowed, 'But she is very good! Why do you need others? Come on, my dear little goddess, chant some more of your vachanas.'

Omkara Shetty was a worried man. When his friend made a snide remark, when the neighbours stared at him and chuckled amongst themselves, he knew Mahadevi had become the centre of gossip in the neighbourhood. Of late Mahadevi visited the matha too frequently and spent long hours there and that too in the company of largely male novices. To complicate matters further, she was careless about her dress. She did not care to plait or tie up her long hair nor cover her breasts properly. It seemed she had no consciousness of her body expected of girls of her age, and behaved like a crazy old woman who had finished with life. And lately, she had developed the habit of standing alone on the banks of the river, either talking to herself, or gazing at the purling river for hours.

'Look, Omkara,' his friend had said, 'I'm not questioning your faith. You know I'm as strong a believer as you are. But that doesn't mean we allow our women to indulge in everything they take fancy to. You know that girl of yours is a little too much. She's breaking all customs and rules and setting a bad example to other girls. I don't know how you allowed her to go this far. You have given her too much freedom. You must do something. If something is wrong with her head, why don't you take her to a healer?'

A sense of regret swept over Shetty. It was surely a blunder to have left Mahadevi unmarried for so long. He shouldn't have agreed to send her to the matha in the first place. But who knew she would change so much and so drastically. And suddenly it seemed to him that there was an element of truth in what his wife had said. The ghost of her notorious grandmother must have really got into her. Omkara decided it was time he took control.

And it so happened that evening, on reaching home he again found Mahadevi not home yet and he shouted at his wife. 'Woman,' he said, 'see what your daughter has brought us to.'

Lingamma sensed what was coming. 'Don't speak like that,' she snapped. 'Remember, she is Shiva's blessing; and you'll not utter a word about this idle gossip to her. These people are all out of their minds. I must tell you, this is all plain jealousy. Our daughter is too intelligent and too beautiful and that these people can't stomach.'

Mahadevi was indeed very beautiful. So beautiful that, as they say, you have to wash your hand before you touch her! Oh, she was fit to be married to a prince. With her strange beauty and her unusually long curly hair that trailed down to almost her knees, she stood out like a little goddess in a crowd.

But that is what actually troubled Omkara Shetty: her beauty. It was like keeping a pot of gold at home and shielding it from thieves. How long could he keep her at home and protect her? It was a terrible burden he wanted to get rid of sooner than later. Something had to be done and done quickly. With no help coming from his wife, he approached Guru Lingadeva for advice. The guru listened to him and, after what seemed a long, thoughtful pause, said, 'Mahadevi is different, Omkara. Just let her be. This distinction between man and woman is artificial and false. These norms and rules of behaviour are man-made and they may be necessary for a social order, but they do not hold good for persons like Mahadevi.'

'It's all right for you to speak that way,' Omkara said, barely able to control himself. 'But I'm a family man and I live amidst people like me. And I have a business to run. I can't break the norms of the society, and I see no reason why I should. Look at other girls, they don't behave like Mahadevi, they don't come to the matha and spend long hours...'

'Don't judge her by comparing her with other girls. She is different.'

'But why should she be so abnormally different? I simply don't understand,' Omkara cried in frustration and then, overcome with remorse, he bemoaned, 'I think it's my fault that I gave her too much freedom.'

A spasm of anger twitched on the guru's face. 'Omkara,' he said sharply, 'if you think she is spoilt because of the freedom you gave her, you are wrong. And if you think she is what she is today because of my teaching or my influence, you are wrong again.'

The conversation was leading nowhere. Finally, almost tearfully, Shetty said what actually he had come to say, 'Kindly do me a favour. Tell her to get married.' And he lied, 'I have already seen a boy for her. If you advise her well, she'll accept.'

'I'll try,' said the guru resignedly, although he knew it would be improper on his part as a guru to force Mahadevi into marriage. True enough, Mahadevi made him regret his words.

'How could you?' she said, quivering with anger she could not express. 'This advice of yours goes against all that you have taught me.'

Returning home in rage, she warned her father, 'If you speak of my marriage again, I'll leave home.'

'Don't speak like that to me,' Omkara yelled. 'You wouldn't be here if your mother and I were not married.'

Mahadevi did not react, just glared at her father in silent fury.

'What then do you want to do?' shouted Omkara. 'Become a jangama?'

'Father,' Mahadevi replied, quietly but firmly, 'I'm already married. Lord Chennamalikarjuna is my husband. I belong to Him, and only Him.'

Devara Dasimayya

In his bundle of clothes, Bahurupi carried seven turbans of seven different colours. Seven is a mystic number. There are seven chakras, energy centres, in the human body, just as there are seven heavenly bodies and seven notes to the musical scale and seven colours in the rainbow. There are seven sages, saptarishis, who keep a close watch on human affairs and from time to time set down their commentaries on life and death and that which is beyond. Living in samsara when you desire to take a life partner, you take seven steps round the sacred fire to enter wedlock. And if and when you come upon disgust with samsara, renouncing your family and all worldly ties, you climb seven hills to reach Kadali, the forest of nothingness. It is said that the Buddha passed seven-night watches to reach nirvana. It took seven days for Allama to come out of the agony over the sudden death of his wife and die to his ego consciousness. Basava developed six steps to reach Shiva, to come upon union with the Infinite Absolute. Six ways of disengagement with the world of samsara and engagement with the ways of the Lord. He missed the seventh step, the one beyond separation and union. However, our Bahurupi, both in awe and in love with the mystic number seven, wore seven different rainbow colour turbans, one on each day of his performance.

That night he wore a blue turban and looked a scorching sun in a dark sky. And he spoke like a driving wind that uprooted trees. 'Devara Dasimayya is our father,' he declared, as if it was an indisputable fact. 'Dasimayya is the one who brought the Linga to our land and established the supremacy of our Lord on earth. He was a great devotee of Lord Shiva, whom Sri Rama worshipped on the banks of the river Cauveri, before he proceeded down South to vanquish the evil Ravana.

'At quite an early age Dasimayya left home and performed fierce tapasya in a forest. He attained such stillness of mind and body that a huge anthill grew over him, and his tapasic heat began to trouble the world and even the gods in heaven. Impressed with his penance, Shiva came down and spoke to him:

'O, bhakta, I am impressed. But why do you punish your body and waste your energy thus. Know that you cannot escape from karma. To live is to perform karma, to act, to work. That is kayaka. Performing action, through kayaka, you shall reach me.'

'And that's how our Dasimayya returned to the world and became a weaver. We call him Jedara Dasimayya because he wove not only soft and fine clothes to cover the bodies of our people, but also knitted blazing vachanas to awaken their minds. Now listen to our Dasimayya.

> *To the one united with Shiva,*
> *there's no dawn, no new moon,*
> *no noonday, nor equinoxes,*
> *nor sunsets, nor full moons.*
> *His kayaka is the worship,*
> *his front yard the holy space.*

'Wielding the sword of his fervent devotion to Shiva, Dasimayya challenged and won over the hearts of Jains and Buddhists. He converted the forest dwellers who lived on animal flesh to non-violent ways of living and earning their livelihood. He admonished the orthodox Brahmins for their meaningless Vedic rituals, their inhuman caste practices and their pedantic nonsense.

> *Did the breath of the mistress*
> *have breasts and long hair?*
> *Or did the master's vital breath*
> *wear sacred thread?*
> *Did the outcaste, last in line,*
> *hold with his outgoing breath*
> *the mark of his tribe?*
> *What do the fools of this world know*
> *of the snares you set and the tricks you play,*
> *O Ramanatha?*

'Thus, with Shiva's trident of fiery wisdom, Dasimayya demolished the decadent traditional distinction between jnana and bhakti, between moksha and samsara, and established the integral yoga of our Lord Shiva.

'Brothers and sisters, our father, Devara Dasimayya, performed these noble acts many decades ago. His was the voice and the way of our Lord. He rebuked the sanyasis and laughed at their barren celibacy. Samsara is not the opposite of spirituality and freedom, he declared. He married Duggale, a pious devotee of Shiva, and lived like an ordinary man in the world. O, he was a spiritual master of the highest order, yet he worked as a weaver and earned his living like any other common man. Kayaka, work, was his mantra and the art of engagement with the visible and invisible world of the Lord.

'You have heard of the famous Jaina King Jayasimha of the Chalukya dynasty and his beautiful wife, Suggale. This beautiful yet mature and knowledgeable queen, Suggale, inspired by our Dasimayya, became a devotee of Shiva, soon to be followed by the king himself. The king and all his family members received initiation into the Shaiva faith from Dasimayya. And you should note this with pride in your hearts: seven hundred Jaina temples were converted into Linga temples, and hundreds of thousands of Jains became Shiva bhaktas.'

A crescent moon stood behind the audience, still and attentive, like a devotee with joined palms, as Bahurupi narrated the story of the life and times of Dasimayya. And then when he narrated with dramatic effect the many miracles Dasimayya had performed, such as bringing a dead boy back to life and transforming serpents into lingas, the crowd went into raptures, chanting the name of our Lord Shiva.

Just as the chanting died down and Bahurupi winded up his story to a wild cheering of his audience, the drum beats started somewhere at the back. And then, clad in a long white robe that accentuated his long black locks dancing about his shoulders, smiling widely like a river, Nageya Marithande came on the stage, carrying his now famous stick and tabor drum. He waved the stick several times in the air as if to drive away ghosts only he could see, banged hard the drum three times as if to rap the audience for their gullibility and awaken them to their senses, and then, without any prelude, he started to tell his story.

'In the city of Kalyana lived a devotee of Shiva called Lingachari. He was hailed as the greatest devotee because of his fierce and total devotion to the Lord. He was truly a wonder to watch and speak to. He spoke only of Shiva and His glory. The name and glory of our Lord vibrated on his burning lips through day and night. He dreaded sleep, for he believed sleep would separate him from his Lord. It is of course a pity that his wife left him, complaining bitterly that he disturbed her sleep and made her life miserable. She was an ignorant fool, but that is another story.'

The crowd broke into giggles and laughter, Nage paused for them to settle down and then continued.

'Lingachari wore six lingas around his neck like a garland, the six lingas representing the six phases a devotee has to negotiate in order to reach the abode of our Lord. Oh, he was a passionate campaigner and champion of our faith, so much so that, once, in a convention of devotees at Kalyana, they even gave him a medal for converting the highest number of bhavis into Shiva bhaktas.

'One day, this redoubtable, the one and only Lingachari, was sitting under a street-side tree, chanting of course the name of our Lord, while his sharp eyes surveyed the people promenading up and down the street. Suddenly his eyes were drawn to a strange-looking man coming down the street. He was as dark as the monsoon clouds, with ash smeared all over his body and limbs. His hair, matted and gnarled, looked like dark serpents slithering down his head. He carried a long stick and looked like one from the cremation ground. He moved languidly, looking this way and that, curiosity written all over his childlike face. He was evidently new to the place and so our rank devotee promptly leapt to his feet and approached the man.

"Who are you?" asked Lingachari, giving a pause to his chanting.

'Startled, the stranger eyed the devotee with some apprehension and then smiled dimly.

"Are you new to Kalyana? Are you a Shiva bhakta?"

'The stranger only smiled as a reply and it seemed the poor fellow was robbed of speech.

"Do you know where you have come? This is the city of gods..." and the devotee launched into the history of the place.

'The stranger, his staff planted by his side, was all ears.

"Come," said the devotee, and dragged the man to the spot under the tree. There, seated on soft grass, looking compassionately at the stranger, the devotee remarked, "Look at you! You look like a moron, like one sunk deep in ignorance!'

'Stretching his lips wide, the stranger smiled like a moron.

"You need to be saved, and the only way you can be saved is through our Lord Shiva. Listen now, and listen closely," said the devotee as a prelude, and then began a long discourse on the eight jewels of the faith and the six virtuous steps to realization.

The stranger listened quietly, but the way he blinked his eyes now and then indicated that he had difficulty in understanding much of what the devotee was saying. Nevertheless, our devotee went on without a pause, like a horse gone wild, and when he finished, he smiled with satisfaction at his own fine performance, and stood up. He picked up his pitcher, and sprinkled the holy water from it on the stranger. 'Salutations to Lord Mahesvara—who has a garland of serpents around the neck; who has three eyes; whose body is covered with vibhuti; who is eternal; who is pure; who has the entire sky as His dress...'

He chanted thus the Shiva stotra in a rather shrill voice and then ordered the stranger to stand up. As the stranger got up obediently, though looking a little dazed, the devotee removed a linga from his garland of six lingas and put it around the neck of the stranger. Then he stepped close to the man and whispered the sacred mantra into his ear.

"Blessings to you, my dear brother," he declared. "From now on you are a Shiva bhakta and one of us."

'The stranger's face grew wide like a huge lotus and it seemed he was supremely happy and felt truly blessed.

"I forgot to ask your name," said the devotee and then scratching his head and grinning, "Oh, I know, you cannot speak. But it's all right."

"I am Shiva," replied the stranger, softly, almost hesitantly, speaking for the first time.

"Naughty fellow!" guffawed Lingachari. "So you tried to fool me, eh? But what a fine name your parents have given you, the importance of which you were foolish enough not to realize till now. Anyway, blessings to you, Shiva, and don't forget to chant the mantra I gave you."

'As the stranger turned, feeling the tiny linga between his fingers and wondering at its smooth surface, Lingachari shouted, "Where are you going, friend? Don't you want to go round and see the city of gods, meet with our gurus and share a meal with us?"

"You are kind," said Shiva in a slow, deep voice. "I have seen and heard enough for a day," he added with a smile, and the next moment he was gone like a bird into thin air.

'The devotee gurgled with self-congratulation, and decided that he was hungry and deserved a good meal at one of the free-meal centres for spiritual mendicants.'

Prabhudeva

His search was at an end. There was nowhere to go, nothing more to know. For the past seven days, with dishevelled hair and torn clothes, he had wandered about the the outskirts of villages and towns like a deranged man, avoiding human contact. He looked emaciated, but he felt no hunger; and even the will to survive seemed to be ebbing away, not to speak of desires. And yet, feeling exhausted as he lay at the foot of a tree, images from his past, images of his parents, his guru and friends, and of his wife, Kamalathe, invaded his mind, like a tidal wave. Where do these images arise from? He wondered. Are my parents still waiting for me? Are they still alive? Then the thought of Kamalathe burned tears through his eyes and he was surprised at himself. 'Life is so much memory!' he thought to himself and smiled, a tired, wan smile.

He looked around. It was only then the details of the landscape began to register in his mind. The trees around stood tall with great dignity, and it seemed, gazing upon him with some strange benignity. Looking up he noticed, through the awning of branches overhead, the sky turning dark grey. Somewhere behind the forest the sun had began his descent into the nether world. Suddenly, something scurried past him and his heart skipped a beat. He sighed and smiled at his own animal fear. But he was not afraid. Some wild creature may come this way and devour him. So be it, he told himself. Life lives on life. In death is peace and an end to all search and doubt and suffering. He had travelled long and now had reached the end of the road. He was finished; there was nothing more to do, his will was at an end.

And then it happened. He felt numb, his limbs turned stiff and cold; it was as if ice-cold water was coursing through his body. He began to gasp; it seemed something was sucking the air out of his lungs. He felt dizzy and he let himself go, like a wounded animal surrendering to death. It was death: the claws of death getting into him. He stretched his limbs and waited, to meet with death. It was strange and funny.

He was not dying! Certainly not dead! For something in him was awake, intensely awake, watching, witnessing everything with a bemused smile, as it were. Was it all just a hallucination? Was it the fear of death playing tricks on him? His body shook, as if invaded by some monstrous wave of energy. Then he felt a thick, fluid darkness slowly envelop him—whether it descended from the sky or emanated from the trees or slipped out of his own eyes, he could not say. Suddenly, it was dark: utterly dark above the clutching hand, dark over the seeing eye, dark over the remembering heart, dark everywhere...

The quest for truth began rather early in Prabhudeva's life. Even as a boy he was full of probing questions and he sought to know everything. He would break flower buds and pull out petals to see what was inside. He would sit in the kitchen in front of the burning fuel and study the flame changing shape and colour; and observe rice cooking, froth breaking, rice grains swelling and turning soft. He would climb up to the terrace of his house and lie down there, staring up at an overcast sky to see the first raindrops. Once, in the early hours, carrying an oil lamp into the garden, he sat by a flower plant to see the bud unfold its petals. Burning with curiosity, nagged by doubts and questions, he would ask his father about God, and how God came into existence, what was beyond the earth, beyond the sky, and beyond the beyond. It was like an absorbing game, but at the end of it all he always felt frustrated and cheated. It seemed he was fed with lies, surrounded by falsehood, and he became angry at everything and everyone.

Once, because Prabhu broke the strings of a veena—a treasured string instrument inherited from a famous musician grandfather—his father scolded and hit him with a stick. In rage, Prabhu snatched the stick from his father and shouted in rage, 'I was only trying to play and I didn't know how to fix the strings. You should have taught me, but instead you beat me. Do you have any sense?' And then he had picked the two-hundred-year-old veena and smashed it to pieces. Never again did the father lose his temper or beat his son.

Nira, Prabhudeva's father, came from a family of musicians who had played and taught music at the king's palace. His mother, Suguna, was the daughter of a courtesan. Nira earned a good wage, often received expensive gifts from the royal family for his services and lived comfortably in a fairly large house. But socially his status was lower than that of a peasant, or a shopkeeper, for he belonged to a caste low in the hierarchy of varnashrama. Even the Brahmin cooks of the palace, who earned less than him, avoided all social interaction with him. In disgust, Nira became a Shaivite.

After his conversion to Shaivism, Nira noticed to his great, pleasant surprise, that even the royal family members treated him with respect he had not enjoyed before. The new faith gave him a higher status and dignity in society. And there was a turnaround in the equation between him and the Brahmins. It was not Brahmins, but he, as a Shiva bhakta, with the sacred ash mark on his forehead, who now felt superior to them.

Ironically, despite his newly found confidence and position in society, this gifted musician did not want his son to learn music; he did not want him to become another glorified slave in the palace. Let the long musical tradition of his forefathers come to an end with him, he often thought, though not without feeling guilty. Prabhu of course was not drawn to music, but he was not averse to it either. Among the collection of drums at home Prabhu took a liking to a small one, a tabor drum, made with goat skin heads and tied to a wooden frame with hemp rope. When his father was away, and when the sun grew soft and pleasant and birds chirped merrily in the trees, he would play the drum, sitting in the backyard.

It was his mother who taught him to play the drum. The day he asked her to teach him to play the drum, she was beside herself with joy. Not because he showed interest in music, but because he had asked her for a favour. Prabhu was fiercely independent even as a boy and sought or expected nothing from others, not even affection. He was never a child to his mother and it hurt her deeply. Any show of affection somewhat irritated him. At times he would be exceedingly jaunty and bubbly and affectionate, but one could never tell how long he would be in such a mood.

Nira was somewhat relieved at Prabhu's apparent indifference to music. And when Prabhu wanted to join the matha to learn Sanskrit and study the scriptures, he readily gave his consent. The arrangement suited both the father and son. The father had been quite worried about Prabhu's utter lack of interest in learning any skill other than reading philosophical texts or loafing around the town the whole day. On Prabhu's part, he was quite happy to be away the whole day and return home only for the night meal and sleep.

At the matha, however, he blossomed into a fine student. He was a fast learner. His sharp mind and ability to absorb and critically reflect upon what he had heard or read impressed his guru. His command over both Kannada and Sanskrit amazed even the pandits. He was awfully bright and brilliant, and he did sometimes make even his teachers feel small and inadequate. When this exceptional student wanted to borrow the ancient texts, the guru, Shivacharya, breaking the matha rule, lent him the texts composed on the delicate palmyra leaves. Prabhu became a voracious reader. His hunger for knowledge took him out of the town to other mathas and ashrams, to even the Jain, Buddhist and Brahmanical learning centres to acquaint himself with their philosophical traditions.

For three years he travelled from one centre to another, meeting Gurus and learning about different sects and their philosophies. And then there came a point when a sort of intellectual fatigue set in and he no more felt the urge to learn anything. It seemed he was going round and round in circles and reaching nowhere. A peculiar rage grew within him against all beliefs and concepts. One day, his Guru Shivacharya confronted him with a barrage of questions. Prabhu's visits to the matha had become few and far between and the guru was naturally curious to know the result of his extensive investigations.

Prabhu was harsh and rude and rather disdainful of all cults and their discourses. He growled out his answers and appeared to be in a hurry to finish the conversation. In utter scorn, which shocked the guru, he dubbed Vedas nonsensical, Upanishads romantic poetry, Jainism escapism, Buddhism negative, and Adi Sankara a fool.

The guru looked stunned. He asked, 'Prabhu, why do you speak thus?'

'I'm just answering your questions.'

'Why do you call Sankara a fool? Don't you think he deserves some respect? You should know that he was no ordinary soul.'

'He may be revered as a great spiritual master but that is secondary to me,' replied Prabhu, rather impatiently. 'What I can't accept is how this man could talk of *Brahman* and the oneness of reality and yet go round writing devotional verses and building temples and establishing mathas? I suspect his *Brahman* was only a concept, at best a deep yearning, and not *anubhaava*, unmediated experience, otherwise he couldn't have gone round composing those texts and doing what he did. And he couldn't have kept quiet about the cruelty and absurdity of varnashrama. His life does not reflect his philosophy of non-dualism. In point of fact, his advaita philosophy itself is problematic. I question his theories, in particular his theory about the two levels of truth. It is not merely a contradiction in terms, but sheer absurdity. How can there be levels to truth? Either it is one or it is nothing. Then his ridiculous theory of maya!'

The guru gestured him to stop. 'Prabhu, don't come to such hasty conclusions,' he said curtly. 'There is some good in all systems and philosophies...'

Without letting the guru finish, Prabhu said, 'I'm not interested in treading a middle path of either the Buddhists or Sankara. It's an attitude of compromise, of defeat. And I don't think we should be afraid to judge others so long as we are ready and willing to be judged by others.'

'Why are you so angry?' asked the guru. 'And what is it you are angry about?'

'I feel cheated, deceived,' Prabhu said in a voice that truly bristled with rage. 'What these traditions and gurus are saying is not true to my experience, not true to my life. They are all false!'

With some hesitation and dreading Prabhu's likely belligerent reaction, the guru persisted, 'Are you saying even our gurus, our ways are not good enough?'

'No,' replied Prabhu too quickly to Shivacharya's comfort. 'I'm not satisfied, not convinced. There seems to be something lacking and I can't put my finger on it. I really don't know, but I want to find out, find out for myself and by myself.'

Shivacharya lost his celebrated cool. 'Prabhu, what is your experience?' he asked sternly. 'You are still a novice. Simply because you have read some texts and learnt some philosophy and has had some experience, you shouldn't think too much of yourself. This *aham* will not take you anywhere. There is so much to learn, so much more to experience and know. You must learn to be humble.'

Prabhu nodded, now looking repentant and thoughtful. 'I agree,' he said, his voice breaking, like a dry twig. 'What I posses is only knowledge, merely what others have said and not my own, not my experience. I know that.' He paused, looking confused and lost, and then abruptly he started again, 'Your questions provoked the answers I gave you, but they are not really the answers at all. You should excuse me if I sounded too harshly judgemental and stupidly arrogant. I wanted to say this in the beginning and I'll say it now. I'm not happy with myself, not satisfied with what I have done or achieved so far. It's nothing, really. I want to know, not in my mind, but in the very flesh and bones of my being what this is all about. And I want to go, leave everything.'

Stunned, the guru did not speak for a while. Then, cautiously, he queried, 'Leave everything! Are you thinking of leaving the matha?'

'Leave the matha, family—everything,' answered Prabhu in a terribly charged tone. 'I don't know, I just want to leave and go where my feet take me. I have no destination in mind.'

Caressing his beard, the guru gave a long sigh, as if to say he knew it would all come to this. He knew Prabhu was not the type who would stay for long under any guru or matha. He had seen the maverick in him the day he had come to the matha eight years ago.

Prabhu sat staring at the guru, expecting him to say something. But the guru only stared back, now with a sense of awe at his one-time disciple. Cross-legged, back erect, Prabhu sat in padmasana. There was a peculiar glow in his eyes, and his long hair, thick moustache and beard gave him the look of a young mystic.

That night, when his parents were asleep, Prabhu stood out gazing at the half-dark. In the search for truth, relationships are irrelevant, rather a burden to be discarded. Sentiments don't matter. Still, before leaving he thought he would see his mother one last time. He went in and watched her fast asleep in the faint moonlight that trickled through the window. Should he wake her and seek her blessing? But she could make it difficult for him to leave. A tear glistened in his eye; he sighed. Nothing is permanent.

He came out of the room with a heavy heart, picked his tabor drum that had become something like a bosom friend, and slipped out into the half-dark. He made his way out of the town under a half-moon that stood at the centre of the sky, with a single thought in his mind: 'I should know, I'll know. And when I know I'll be a new man.'

Thus, renouncing his family and the matha, with fire in his heart, Prabhu walked with long strides, as if in a hurry to reach his destination.

For the next three years Prabhu travelled across the country with no particular goal in mind. He travelled through the day and broke journey on reaching some village in the evening. There, as night descended on the land and lamps were lit inside homes, he would plant himself in the village square, play his drum and sing hymns he had picked up from his mother, or chant vachanas he had learnt over the years at the matha. It usually fetched him food and shelter for the night. The next day, at the crack of dawn, he would be gone without bothering to inform even his host. As days passed, the news spread that a holy man with a golden voice was travelling through the land, offering spiritually elevating devotional songs and vachanas, and that he was a strange jangama, with no name and affiliation to any tradition or order.

This is a ridiculous way of living, Prabhu would sometimes tell himself, but something in him would urge him to let go of things: 'Let it be, let me flow with the tide and not resist anything.' Like wind changing direction from time to time, like a fakir, he travelled from village to town and village to village. Once he did meet with a fakir in one of the villages he stopped by. Just when he had finished a song, a middle-aged bearded man came out of the crowd and then moving over to where Prabhu stood with his drum, he began to sing in a loud, sonorous voice. As Prabhu started playing his drum to the rhythm of the song, the fakir, in an apparent state of ecstasy, broke into a dance. Moving his arms rhythmically, he danced as he sang and sang as he danced within a small imaginary circle. Slowly the crowd began to chant: *Allaha-o-Allalaha-bisimillaha*...Fascinated, as Prabhu kept playing his drum, the fakir broke into yet another dance and song:

> *I know not who I am:*
> *I am not a believer resting in*
> *a mosque or a temple,*
> *neither a saint nor a sinner,*
> *neither a man nor a woman.*
> *I belong to no country, no state.*
> *I am no Moghul, no Hindu, nor a Turk.*
> *I know only this that*
> *I am none and everyone,*
> *I am the beginning and the end.*
> *I am who calls himself:*
> *The Nameless One.*

❖ ❖ ❖

In the early hours, as was his practice, Prabhu left the village and at dawn entered the land of Banavasi. It seemed like a realm in heaven with pleasing soft-blue sky, enchanting green everywhere, murmuring streams and majestic trees. It was springtime and the verdant land sparkled with flowers of various hues. A poet could not but be gay in such an enchanting surrounding and sing in celebration of the great beauty. Strangely, Prabhu had not so far composed a single vachana of his own. Enthralled by the splendour of nature, he now tried to sing, but words failed him.

However, a strange feeling enveloped his being and he felt as if floating in the air. He had never felt so light and frivolous before. Something had changed. On entering the town he was further dumbfounded by the tall and large buildings and the many gardens he passed by. The streets were surprisingly broad and well maintained. The street he took led him to the huge and magnificent Madhukeshwara temple. Entering the spacious square, he was struck by the soaring stambha, the intricately laid stones and the towering pagoda that carried motifs of devas and rakshasas and celestial nymphs.

Feeling refreshed after a wash in the nearby stream, Prabhu sat on the steps of the temple, watching the never-ending stream of devotees eager to offer their puja and seek the blessings of Lord Madhukeshwara. Suddenly, there was a hush everywhere, and he saw a young woman, dressed in royal attire, enter the square, followed by pretty looking women carrying coloured umbrellas and golden plates filled with things to be used for puja. The temple bell chimed continually as the priest chanted mantras from inside the sanctum sanctorum. Prabhu kept watching the people around him with keen eyes and then, slowly, his attention was drawn to a girl who stood behind a pillar inside the hall of the temple. Her palms folded and raised to eye-level, she appeared to be immersed in prayer, but to Prabhu's huge surprise, he caught her throwing occasional furtive glances at him with a slight tilt of her head. That moment Prabhu forgot the surroundings and his past. He felt his body grow warm and his heart swell with feelings he had never felt before. Without taking his eyes off her, he stood up and, like an animal in heat, began to climb the steps of the temple. On entering the hall, he broke into a song. He played the drum as he sang, and, as if moved by some unseen force, he began to dance. He danced as he sang and sang as he danced within a small imaginary circle.

He did not know her name, or her background; nor did he care to. She was young and beautiful: like irrediscent sunset clouds in summer. She was every woman desired by every man. She was she and he was he, waiting to meet and unite with her from primordial times. It was love without thought, desire without shame. They rode on the high tide of passion without fear or thought of the morrow. Either in the morning or evening, depending upon his mood, he sang and danced at the temple. The performance earned him enough silver to rent a house and meet the household expenses. They made love by day and made love by night. It seemed their hunger for each other would never be fulfilled.

After three months of their living together, one morning, she woke up shivering. It was as if the fires of the world had invaded her body. No vaidya, no medication was of help. On the sixth day, as the full moon stood high over the hills and a soft wind came in from the river, her body turned cold and still. 'You cannot die on me…,' Prabhu kept wailing, refusing to get up from her side. 'She's dead,' the physician reiterated patiently, feeling for the young man. 'She's alive, she'll wake up soon and you'll see it,' Prabhu screamed, pushing the physician away. And when the neighbours came in to move the body to the burial ground, he yelled at them and drove them out. Moaning and muttering to himself, cursing and praying, hot tears streaming down his cheeks, his hair dishevelled, half-naked, Prabhu sat by Kamalathe's lifeless body the whole night. In the faint glow of the lamp placed near her head, with unblinking eyes he watched her face, looking for signs of life. The miracle did not happen. And something in him began to die, too. Next morning, as the first rays of the sun crept through the lone window and washed over the putrefying corpse, Prabhu rose like one from a state of trance, as if someone had rudely woken him.

Prabhu sat up with a start. Everything had changed. It seemed the forest was lit up with a thousand suns. There simply was too much light: burning, relentless. And yet, he noticed with growing wonder that he could, as if from close, see everything, be it a stone, a blade of grass or a bush, in all its intricate details. Everything he beheld was suffused with light. He looked up now and saw that the tall trees were on fire. But this strange light or fire had a cool presence about it. It was as if the trees were made of water, reflecting fire raging in some place afar.

Am I alive? He asked and felt fear grip him. Maybe I'm dying and this is what happens when one is passing out, or maybe I'm already dead and this is how the world, the reality becomes visible again after death, he thought. It all seemed funny and yet something in him was scared to let things go.

For seven days he had wandered aimlessly from place to place, like a dry leaf blown hither and thither. He had flitted across towns and villages, valleys and woods, like a shrinking shadow. In villages and towns, through which he had passed only a few months before as a wandering singer and monk, nobody recognised him, nor did he remember them. Once, by a river he had stopped and watched a huge pyre burst in flames, and in the swirling blaze and smoke the mourning kith and kin of the burning body who had been once a man, and he had burst into a hoarse laughter. And then, deep inside forests, he had come upon seekers engaged in penance, and he had howled: 'There is no God, no truth, no reality, no self, nothing beyond…'

He had drifted like a mad man, roaring with laughter, but with doubts and questions still burning in his head: Who is this laughing? And what is this suffering I feel deep in my heart? Who is suffering? How do I know this is suffering? Is this pain, or is it joy? Is it all a mere trick of memory? Is there anything beyond memory? The traditional answers to these questions were no answers at all. He brushed them all aside only to face a blank wall for an answer. But he could not go on for long. With no answer coming, his head grew tight and unyielding, like a nut refusing to crack. He was that hard nut, that question: Who is asking these questions? What is this 'I'? There was no answer. He had wandered with that single question burning through his entire being. Burning, crackling, like *arani* sticks.

He stood up and started moving, as one steered by some invisible force. It was strange. He felt as if he was floating through a tunnel of light. Now he saw, at a distance, a hill, not so much a hill as a pyramid of light piercing the sky. Soon, he found himself on the fire hill and in front of a cave that looked like a shimmering water hole. Something had brought him here and he knew why. This is where he would breathe his last, inside the cave. And everything will be over and done with. There was now no fear, only acceptance of the inevitable. There was no question, no will left in him. It all seemed so simple and easy, and there was such grace. It was a blessing. He entered the cave and that is all he remembered. A towering column of fire burned brightly. It was huge, immense, without base or middle or end; it was immeasurable. And there was such compassion about this pillar of flame; it was not kindness, not the opposite of anything; it was untouched by thought. Prabhu did not know if he was witnessing this great fire or he was himself the infinite, timeless flame. Like a river in spate, his consciousness was breaking through the time-worn barriers; and then time ceased to exist.

It could have been after several days, or several ages, when Prabhu finally emerged from the cave—he looked like burnished gold. The first thought that occurred to him was: how can I speak of what cannot be spoken, what do I do now?

'You'll know what to do,' said a voice. 'Things will happen, things will come to you. It's no more a matter of choice.'

In front of him stood the fakir from the village where Prabhu had spent the night singing and playing the drum.

'I can see that you know,' continued the man with the long beard and large, penetrating eyes. 'You have seen, and it's there in your eyes.'

Prabhu smiled and vachanas poured forth from his burning lips:

> *I saw the toad swallow the sky,*
> *the blind man catch the snake.*
> *I saw the heart conceive,*
> *the hand grow big with a child,*
> *the ear drink up the smell of camphor,*
> *the nose eat up the dazzle of pearls, and*
> *hungry eyes devour diamonds.*
>
> *In a blue sapphire,*
> *I saw the three worlds hiding.*
> *Yet, looking for your light,*
> *I went hither and thither,*
> *in and out, and it was like*
> *a sudden dawn of*
> *a million million suns,*

> *a ganglion of lightings,*
> *O Lord of the Caves.*
> *But tell me,*
> *if you are light, what am I?*
> *O, there can be no metaphor...*

The bearded one folded his palms and bowed in a gesture of both greeting and obeisance.

'Words are deceptive,' Prabhu spoke, addressing the fakir. 'They hide more than they reveal, and they are shy and dangerous! The word, in fact, is the world, and it is a dream.' And he walked past the fakir, who, his palms still joined in reverence, whispered: Allama!

Allama

The fires atop the poles at the four corners of the stage hissed, like the mythical seven-headed serpent. In his dark-yellow turban that shimmered like unalloyed joy, Bahurupi stood at the centre, telling his story.

'One day, I met Allama Prabhu and introduced myself. Mischief glinted in his eyes when I called myself a storyteller. He already knew about me and I felt truly flattered. And then getting on to my business, I begged him for *his* story.

'He laughed a laugh that was at once mocking and affectionate. He said, "Sorry, there's no story."

'But you know I'm not the type who would take such a reply for an answer. I'm like a gravedigger, who'll not stop digging until he finds something to play with. So, as I kept persisting and pestering him with questions, and at last, Prabhu asked, "How will you tell a story? When and at what point does a story begin, eh? There is no point. Forget it. You do not know, you cannot know."

'I said, "Prabhu, you are destroying the very ground on which my living is based. You should not be so unkind. Give me a clue or something with which I can begin."

'He stopped me with a wave of his hand, and said, "When the sky is the palmyra leaf and wind the story, what will you say and where will you begin?"

'I said, "Prabhu, that is a beautiful metaphor!"

'He said, "All stories are metaphors in frames of time and space."

'I said, "So at least you agree there are stories, though we may not know where and how to begin."

'Laughing, he gurgled, "Stories within stories within stories, eh? You are a charming liar."

'I said, "Prabhu, I tell stories to make a living and pass my time. I have no other talent, you see."

'"That's all right," he said, with an approving smile. "Go and tell your stories. But remember, you really cannot tell the full story of anyone or anything, not even your own, let alone of someone called Allama."

'So you see, brothers and sisters, Allama has to negate everything. His very name, *Allama, Allayya, Alla*, means 'no', 'not it'; he is the first and last negator of everything that can be expressed. Sometimes I wonder if he is a person, a human being at all. What I mean is: he is an enigma!

'No. He'll himself not tell his story, ever. And that's why for every Allama a Bahurupi and Nage are born to tell the untold story. But then, as Allama would warn, we cannot tell the full story of anyone or anything, for every story is a part of another that has gone before, like every beginning is already the second.'

Amongst the women sat Mahadevi, listening and watching Bahurupi with unblinking eyes. From morning she had been excited on knowing that both Bahurupi and Nage were in town and that they would be performing in the evening. She was there now, sitting in the front row, trying to make sense of what Bahurupi was saying. There were murmurs of approval and grumbles of disapproval, and she heard a woman, who was sitting close to her, mutter, 'Sometimes this Bahurupi is really confusing. Why doesn't he just get on with the story?'

Actually, Allama's story was not entirely unknown to the people there. The saranas, who visited the matha, were quite familiar with the lives and vachanas of Devara Dasimayya,

Allama, Basava, Siddarama, and a host of other masters. Still they loved to listen to Bahurupi, for he always brought in something new, something they had not heard before, and they enjoyed the way he narrated these stories giving them his own peculiar twists and turns, interspersed of course with his own, though often confusing and confounding, philosophical commentaries. Mahadevi was hearing him for the first time, and now, she told herself: 'One day I'll meet Allama, and he'll tell me his story.'

Bahurupi continued:

'Mysterious are the ways of Shiva. The web of maya in which we get entangled is His making. Otherwise, you may ask, why would Prabhu fall madly in love with Kamalathe and why would she die even before they could start a family? Was it preordained, or was it his karma and it had to happen to him? What we know is that the beautiful Kamalathe died young. She breathed her last when the moon had come out full, looking amiably over the land. Her death drove Prabhu into despair and then to the ultimate release from all bondage.

'Heart-broken and in terrible grief, Prabhu wandered through the land, but always on the outskirts of towns and villages, avoiding all human contact. And like Shiva who wandered through the Pine Forest, thinking of Sati, our Prabhu, hair dishevelled and ash smeared over his naked body, wandered through the forest of Banavasi, the image of Kamalathe locked in his heart. When he couldn't stand the pang of hunger, he drank water from puddles in forests or swallowed his own saliva, and when sleep crept over him, he fell asleep wherever he sat. Something inside him and of him, the traces, the karmic effect of his past, began to wither and fall to pieces. He no longer had the will to go on, and yet he continued to drift, like a dry leaf blown hither and thither.

'For seven days he moved about in this peculiar state, and on the seventh day, he sat on a huge mound not knowing why he was there. The sun was on the hills, watching Prabhu, and time passed by, like a soft breeze from the river. He felt something wet and a sharp pain shot up his right thigh. He moved to a side and saw something jutting forth from the earth, like the nipple-peak on the breast of mother goddess. Instinctively, as he dug the ground with his fingers around the point, he was surprised to find that it was a golden cupola of a temple buried in the earth. Excited, he found a sharp-edged stone and began digging furiously. Soon, as if under some mysterious force, the earth gave way and a door emerged. Kicking the door open, Prabhu entered the dark, cave-like structure. There, as the sun penetrated through the openings above and lit the inside space, what did Prabhu see?'

The crowd held its breath. Even Guru Lingadeva, who was sitting close to the platform, felt goose bumps on his skin, although he knew what was coming.

'Prabhu beheld, in the heart of the temple, a Yogi, his face aglow, eyes without eyelids, wide open, and a thin smile playing on his thin lips. The next moment, a blinding light burst forth from the body of the yogi, circled the space three times and shot up and out through the opening in the roof. There, in the spot where the yogi, Animishayya, the one without eyelids and open eyes, had sat, Prabhu saw a linga swathed in brilliant light. As Prabhu picked up the linga, with no thought, his mind empty, his body burning like the sun, the light from the sacred linga shot out and passed through his body and he was awakened.

'The one who emerged from the cave was no more the Prabhu of the past, but Prabhu, the master of the eternal present. He was Allama, the one who knows and has seen it all. Allama, in whom the sorrows of the world have come to an end!'

Suddenly, as the drum beats started from somewhere behind him, Bahurupi broke into a dance, and as he danced, Nage came up the stage and sang a couple of Allama's vachanas:

Your Vedas are mere words,
Your shastras and puranas a gossip,
Your bhakti so much noise...

Unless you burn fire, wet water,
Unless you catch wind and conquer the sky,
What can you know of the way of Yoga?

Then, with perfect timing, Bahurupi stepped forward and in a booming voice, resumed the story of Allama's spiritual journey through the land.

'Like the butterfly with no memory of the caterpillar, Allama flew through the untrammelled air, spreading the fragrance of the mystique of enlightenment. He was like a river with a million currents, rushing through the landscape, bringing in its wake a new awakening. Through his technique of mockery, irony, diatribe, profanity and laughter, he taught those who were ready to listen: the art of not-knowing, the non-rationality of love and wisdom, and the trick of *bayalu*, open space, emptiness. To the Kaapalikas he taught the yoga of divine copulation, to the Advaita Vedantins the maya of non-dualism, to the Jains the ahimsa of the mind, and to the Siddhas the magic of nothingness.

'One day, while passing through the land of the Siddhas, he met Goraksha, the Guru of Siddhas. Goraksha stood blocking his path, grinning. His yogic powers were legendary. He was in his sixties but looked a young man in his twenties. Tall, broad shouldered, his body glowed with his yogic powers. He had the power of levitating in the air, walking on water, and travelling on astral plane. He could read the minds of people and predict their future; make the lame walk, and the sick become healthy and energetic. And he had the magical power to produce little objects out of nothing.

'"I can see that there is something about you," said Goraksha to Allama, with a mocking laugh. "But why do you keep yourself thus? Like one who has lost everything in life, like one living on the edge of life?"

'With dishevelled hair, a shaggy beard and in rags, Allama did look like one who was done with life. He said, "You are right. I have lost everything and for good."

'"You pretend," Goraksha guffawed. "It's an act, a trick you put on to impress people. But that'll not work with me. Come on now, show me what you are."

'"I have nothing to show, nothing to prove. There is nothing," said Allama.

'"You are a coward," Goraksha sniggered. "You are scared to challenge me. You might have won your little games over others, but you cannot win over me. So why don't you gracefully accept defeat and I'll let you pass."

'"I'm not interested in playing games, nor am I interested in winning over you or anyone," said Allama, his voice growing tight and severe. "Now get off my path."

'"So you are scared of me," taunted Goraksha, laughing sneeringly and provoking Allama further.

'"What if you fail?" asked Allama, glaring at him.

'"I'll become your disciple and follow you like a shadow."

'"I need no disciples," roared Allama. "You shall follow none."

'And that's how the strange contest between the two masters began. Taking out a deadly sword that shone liquid-white like silver, Goraksha said grimly, "This will be the first of several contests; if you survive this one, that is. Are you prepared?"

'Meeting his gaze, Allama smiled.

'Goraksha handed him the sword and said, "Strike me and cut me in two, if you can. Come on, don't hesitate."

'Allama swung the sword at Goraksha, but the blade only clanged against his body that was hard as diamond. And Goraksha roared in triumph.

'Returning the sword to Goraksha, Allama said, "Try it on me now. Let's see. Don't fear."

'The muscles in Goraksha's arms stood out in knots as he held the sword in a tight grip. He inhaled deeply, and then holding his breath, Goraksha swung the sword at Allama with all his strength. The sword swished through Allama's body, as if through space.

'"You are empty," cried Goraksha, in utter amazement, and his sword fell from his hand and lay near Allama's feet.'

That night, Bahurupi and Nage had one of their rare quarrels. The evening performance at the matha had ended with Nage playing the drum and joining Bahurupi in singing more of Allama's vachanas. But he had not, as was the usual practice, re-entered the stage to entertain the crowd with his customary, humorous tales. 'Your story was long and good enough for the day,' he had told Bahurupi and had walked away. And now, after the meal and sitting on the terrace of the main building of the matha, at last, breaking his silence, Nage asked, 'Did Allama tell you the story you narrated today?'

It was a clear night and the stars were out like devotees at pilgrim centres. But the moon stood at an angle, looking rather lonely. Bahurupi sensed the cause of Nage's mood. But let him say it, he thought. There were evenings when he had felt that Nage's jokes were not only in bad taste, but destroyed the profound effect of his stories on the audience. At such times, burning with rage, he would think that Nage's subversive stories, instead of offering any radical insights into life, only betrayed his cynical attitude towards everything.

However, this occasional, nagging suspicion on the part of Bahurupi had never come in the way of their friendship so far. They had remained good friends and had gone out and performed their roles on stage in perfect unison.

Now, Bahurupi said, 'Didn't you hear what I said in the introductory piece, that Allama said that there was no story and all that?'

'And still you gave them some mythical stuff.'

'Come on, Nage, you are more intelligent than that. People need stories and you should know that telling stories is the only way to preserve the memories of these masters and their teachings.'

'Yes, but not fairy tales,' said Nage.

'Inspiration, my friend,' Bahurupi shouted, getting quite irritated. 'Stories, even what you call fairy tales, inspire people.'

'To what?'

'To preserve an awareness in some corner of their being that this is not all there is to life and that there is something more to what they see and experience.'

'No, they are very misleading,' countered Nage. 'And such imaginary stuff can put people on the wrong path.'

Wrong path! Now this was too much even for a good friend. 'You think you know everything, you know the right path?' Bahurupi challenged. 'Tell me then, what is the right path?'

'I don't know,' Nage replied in anger. 'All I'm saying is that you don't mesmerize people with some magical stuff. What is this story of Goraksha's sword passing through Allama's body as if he were made of space? Did such a thing happen? Can such things really happen? What are you trying to prove? You tell stories to awaken people, not to put them to sleep, my friend.'

'Nage, Nage,' Bahurupi reacted with equal vehemence and anger, 'I don't deal with truths, only with metaphors of truths and realities. I'm not Basava or Allama; I'm only a storyteller telling my stories for a living. And in my own way, I'm a seeker too. A seeker groping through his stories, grappling with things I don't fully understand. But, tell me, what are you? Who do you think you are? And pray, what kind of stories do *you* tell? Are they meant to awaken people?'

'I'll answer you tomorrow,' snapped Nage, and, without uttering another word, went down to his room. The next day, after Bahurupi's performance, Nage entered the stage, wielding his stick like a sword, and laughing like one gone mad. And he narrated another story:

'One day, there was a fierce argument between a bhakta and a bhavi. The two, incidentally, happened to be friends from their childhood. They had married two sisters from the same family and set up their homes in the same locality as neighbours. They never disagreed with each other, never quarrelled. They were like one mind in two bodies, until the day when one of them wore the linga on his body and became a Shiva bhakta, and the other refused to go along with him. Every time they met, they argued and quarrelled over the question of faith. That day, after a sumptuous meal at a Dasoha centre, the two of them came to a park to rest and continue their debate.

'At one point, the bhakta lost his temper and said, 'You saw our saranas, our jangamas, how spiritually dignified and profound they all were. You saw our Guru, the divine glow on his face. You heard his discourse, you ate his food and still you speak like this?'

'I came because I didn't want to disappoint you,' said the bhavi, with a wicked grin. 'Also, to be frank, I thought, where is the harm in joining you for a free meal?'

'You really are disappointing!' The bhakta sighed sadly. 'Brother, I'll tell you this. At last, I have found real meaning and happiness in life. Since we have been with each other as friends, actually like brothers, for so long, I sincerely wished that you too should know and experience this supreme happiness that I know and experience every moment of my life.'

'I'm all right as I am. Why do you want me to tread your path? Why are you being so pushy and fanatical?'

The bhakta gave a short laugh, as if to say he pitied his friend. Then, getting serious and challenging him, he said, 'All right, let's discuss this matter to finish today. Tell me truthfully, what gives you happiness?'

'Needless to say it is the love of my wife and children. What else?' replied the friend, frowning, and then he threw the question back at him: 'Now *you* tell me what gives you happiness?'

The bhakta smiled. 'No, not my family, but the company of other bhaktas, our saranas, gives me supreme happiness!'

'Ah! Good sleep keeps me cheerful,' chuckled the bhavi.

'Chanting of vachanas,' said the bhakta.

And soon it became a sort of verbal game between them.

'Food; good, tasty food,' continued the bhavi.

'The holy water,' responded the bhakta.

'A cool breeze in summer and a warm sun in winter!'

'The kindly gaze of our Guru and his sweet words,' gushed the bhakta, grinning as if he had already scored several points over his friend.

'The eyes of a beautiful woman.'

'The beatific smile of the Guru.'

'Sitting by the lake with no worry in the world.'

'Listening to a jangama's discourse.'

'Ah! Nothing like going into the field to relieve myself. Therein lies my greatest happiness.'

The bhakta burst out laughing. And then suddenly, his face contorted with some unbearable discomfort, and beads of sweat broke out on his forehead.

'What happened, you seem to be in some pain?' asked the bhavi, not without concern.

'My stomach,' confessed the bhakta. 'I think I ate a little too much.' And, screwing up his face, he stood up. The bhavi leapt to his feet and held his friend's hand.

'What are you doing? Wait here, I'll come back soon,' shouted the bhakta.

'No,' said the bhavi, gripping his friend's hand firmly. 'Let's first finish the argument we started. Let's come to some agreement, or, let's at least agree to disagree.'

'Be kind,' pleaded the bhakta, 'I'm in no state to argue. Let me go...'

But the bhavi wouldn't let go of his friend's hand. The pulling and pushing with some harsh shouting thrown in, went on for a while, and then the bhakta started almost crying, 'I beg of you, please let me go. I agree with whatever you say.'

'So now,' the bhavi said, withdrawing his hands and beaming triumphantly, 'tell me, what is the source of happiness?'

'His face cracking in pain, clutching at his stomach, the bhakta turned and dashed towards a bush.'

Only a few in the crowd, mostly women, burst into laughter, while most of the men frowned and grumbled and swore at Nage. And then a couple of overzealous young saranas, getting quite excited and angry, sprang to their feet, cursing and shaking their fists at Nage. Nage stood his ground and shouted back, 'Come on, you want to kill me, kill me for a joke? What kind of bhaktas are you who can't take a joke?'

The situation could have turned into something very unpleasant and even violent if not for Bahurupi, who rushed on to the stage and pulled Nage back. Then addressing the incensed crowd, he pleaded, 'This is only a story, please don't take it so seriously. Sit down, please sit down, we still have not finished.'

Guru Lingadeva had left by then, but, fortunately, there were other senior saranas in the crowd who now intervened and calmed down the agitated young men. Just as the crowd slowly settled down, Nage rushed forward to the edge of the stage and, raising his stick and his voice, said, 'Hush..hush... now listen, and listen carefully. I said it was only a joke, and Bahurupi, my friend, said, it was only a story. What we mean is that every joke is a story and every story a joke, depending of course on how you look at it.'

Bahurupi sensed trouble and was worried. Not everyone was listening to Nage. Some men were still arguing over the story between themselves. It was potentially a dangerous situation. Still, undeterred, Nage went on speaking eloquently, then all of a sudden, he ceased. Before long, beating his drum and waving his stick wildly yet again, he started to dance.

Bahurupi had never seen Nage dance before. He danced to some strange music only he could hear, and then he started to swirl round the stage like a top. It was no dance. It seemed he pirouetted round the stage only to burn up his anger. It was strange and it was weird, but, all the same, the people enjoyed it all thoroughly, clapping their hands and shaking with laughter. Now that he had the crowd hooting with laughter, Nage stopped his tandava as abruptly as he had begun; and, panting for breath, slowly moved to the front of the stage.

He waved his stick as if to drive away menacing spirits and that elicited some more laughter. Then he beat his drum and bellowed, 'It's really good to see you all laughing.

It'll be better still if you learn to laugh at yourself. You must know that a true devotee of Shiva is the one who knows to laugh at oneself. And you must know that if truth is greater than gods, laughter is greater than truth, for in laughter the divine and the human merge, the earth and heaven become one and we are freed from all fear and from all sorrow. That is why the wise one prays, 'May the laughter of Shiva protect us.'

Sighing and smiling with relief, Bahurupi noted that the crowd had grown quiet and attentive. But how long would it last? Another offensive story or wicked joke from Nage, he feared, would surely drive the crowd mad with fury. But mercifully, Nage was singing a different tune. He was saying, 'Have you heard the story of Shiva laughing at himself?'

'Tell us the story, tell us...' the crowd chanted in one voice.

'Hush, listen and listen with all your ears. You know how, in order to win Shiva's love, Parvati performed great penance in the forest?'

'One day, on hearing about her tapasya, Shiva goes to the forest to test her. He goes disguised as a mendicant who has taken the vow of chastity. When Parvati speaks about her intense love for Shiva and her desire to wed him, the mendicant-in-disguise starts laughing. Irritated by the mendicant's reaction, yet in great fervour, Parvati expresses the sincerity of her love. In response, the mendicant begins to make fun of Shiva. As Shiva makes fun of Shiva, and laughs at himself, he says, "O beautiful one, he is no match for you, just forget him. He'll come to the wedding not dressed in fine clothes, or on a royal elephant, as you probably expect, but dressed in elephant hide he'll come riding on his old bull, followed by ghouls and goblins. Imagine him in a mere loin cloth, his body smeared with ash, standing by your side, in your fine, embroidered bridal dress! O how incongruous and absurd it would be! Why should a young and beautiful thing like you marry a disgusting one like Shiva? He has no parents, no family, he is poor; he is three-eyed and to make things worse, smeared with ash he goes around stark naked in the burning grounds. My dear girl, forget him, he is not the kind of husband you would want to live with."

'Making wide eyes, Parvati stares blankly at him.

"Oh, how funny you two would look as a couple!" Shiva persists.

Suddenly, and to her own utter amazement, the remark snaps something inside her and she starts giggling. 'A funny couple!' she mumbles. 'Yes, we two would make an extraordinarily funny couple, and why not?' And she breaks into a lilting laughter, imagining her prospective ash-smeared husband and herself by his side, in fine silk and jewels. A laughter that is at once a rejection of the world's stupid and blinkered opinion of Shiva and acceptance of Shiva in all his avatars. As her ringing laughter swirls around him like an enchanting music, Shiva reveals himself and behold, now both he and Parvati begin to laugh together like they had never laughed before, which soon spreads and infects the heavens and the gods too come out, shaking with laughter. Soon there is a roar, the sky thunders and the heavenly laughter falls on earth, and thus the earth is enriched with the fragrance of the divine laughter.'

Just as a few in the crowd burst into giggles and laughter, and some still kept wondering what to make of the story, Nage broke into a song:

> O Lord, as you laugh and whirl about in dance,
> nectar flows from the moon atop your head,
> drips into the mouths of the skulls around your neck,
> reviving them, and teeth bared, they laugh,
> proud, fierce, wild, apocalyptic laughter,
> shattering the darkness around,
> cleansing heaven and earth.

O Lord, may your laughter protect us,
save us from all fear and sorrow.

No sooner had Nage finished the singing than he started again:

'Now listen, and listen attentively. In the beginning, there was nothing but Prajapati, It, the Self, the primordial being in the form of a person. He looked around and saw that there was no one else, nothing but himself, whereupon his first shout was, 'It is I!' Whence the concept 'I', 'self' arose. Then he was afraid. That is why anyone alone is afraid. But he thought to himself: 'Why this trembling of the self, this fear? Since there is no one here but myself, what is there to fear?' And he started to laugh at his own fear, at himself, and he laughed so long and loud and hard that it burst the darkness of the world and the fear departed.'

Nage paused to let his new, naughty yet good-humoured story of creation sink into the minds of his audience with their mouths open with giggles and guffaws and then, in a commanding voice, he continued, 'Now repeat this mantra, the first-ever mantra uttered by the primordial Prajapati. Repeat after me: *Om-haha-hum, hum-ho-ho, hoho-hum, hee-hee-ho-hum, haha-hee-hee, ha-ha-haaa, hee-hee-heee...*'

While some cheerfully and gleefully chanted after Nage, many in the crowd, including those young saranas who only sometime ago wanted to strangle Nage for his blasphemous story, roared with uncontrollable laughter.

Bahurupi swelled his cheeks and let out a long sigh.

That night, just before going to sleep, he asked, 'Nage, my friend, tell me, what is the source of your joke, your laughter?'

Promptly Nage answered, 'The awareness that we do not know, that we cannot know, that it is not in the realm of knowing.'

'Pray, what is that?'

'We do not know what we are saying, nor do we know what we are doing and what this is all about, yet, we go on as if we know everything and we take everything seriously, rather too seriously, and we begin to look ridiculously funny and thus become the subject and object of laughter...'

Married to God

Mahadevi could not sleep a wink that night. Every cell in her body throbbed with some strange energy; it was as if her body was on fire. 'O Lord,' she cried out, 'I cannot suffer this agony; cut through these worldly knots and take me with you, O Lord Chennamalikarjuna...' And then she saw, as if in answer to her prayer, a tiny dot of light hovering about. Soon, the faint, tiny flame grew into a bright circle and the circle into a fiery ball of flame and it wavered up and down and sideways as if reluctant to go near her. After what seemed an eternity, slowly, the fiery orb started to move towards her. It was blazing hot as if the sun had risen inside the room. The flame inched closer and closer towards her. Suddenly a sharp spasm of energy, like lightening, exploded up her spine and she lost her consciousness.

The next morning, when Mahadevi opened her eyes, she saw her mother sitting by her side, smiling, and tenderly stroking her hair. Sitting up, she flung her arms around her mother and burst into tears.

'What happened, my dear? Did you have a bad dream?' Lingamma asked, patting her back affectionately.

'O mother, I burned in a flameless fire, I suffered from a bloodless wound, I tossed without a moment of relief, I wandered through unlikely worlds.'

It seemed to Lingamma that it was not her daughter speaking, but some strange ethereal voice from inside her. She pulled back and stared at her daughter, somewhat scared. Mahadevi's eyes looked blank, or she was looking at something through and beyond her.

'Tell me, Mahadevi,' Lingamma asked, her heart thudding in fear. 'Did something happen? Tell me.'

Mahadevi said, 'Amma, I want to go; get me married.'

Lingamma smiled; only a moment before she was afraid her heart would stop beating. Now taking her daughter's hands in hers, she said, 'All girls leave their parents' home when they get married. How long can we keep you with us even if we want? Silly girl!' And Lingamma stood up, holding back her tears. 'Your father will be happy to hear that you have agreed to marry,' she said, avoiding Mahadevi's eyes. 'Now get up and take your bath. It is time for the puja.'

'Get me married to Lord Chennamalikarjuna. He shall be my husband.'

Lingamma turned around and stared at her daughter, unsure if she had heard her correctly. Mahadevi was sitting cross-legged on the bed with a straight back, in a meditative posture, as if it was not she who had spoken. Her long, dishevelled hair curled over her shoulders and chest in a mass of tangles, a thin smile played about her face and a peculiar glow shone in her eyes. She looked weird, and beautiful.

'Mad girl!' Lingamma tried to laugh. 'In this real world we marry real men. Now get up and get ready. Don't make your father wait for long.' And she rushed out of the room.

'He shall be my husband,' Mahadevi hummed to herself. 'The One with no clan, no caste, and no family; the One who has no place, no boundary and no origins; the One who knows no death, nor decay...'

It all happened too quickly for Omkara's and Lingamma's liking. An unlikely bridegroom claimed Mahadevi for his wife. He was a bhavi. He was Kaushika, a minor King who ruled over Uduthadi and the surrounding provinces that came under the suzerainty of the emperor Bijjala of Kalyana, under whom Basavanna served as a minister.

That day, when the family had set out to a nearby Shiva temple, King Kaushika was on his way to the next town. Mahadevi's two friends, the dark and charming Prabhavati and the slim and beautiful Sukanya, were going to the temple with her. They were meeting her after a long time. Prabhavati had come to her parent's house for the birth of her child. Sukanya, married for three years and with a child, was visiting her parents. Both friends talked in tandem, filling Mahadevi's ears with endless family anecdotes. Mahadevi smiled occasionally, listening and not listening to their continuous chatter, and once gently pinched the little one's cheek. Unlike other girls she felt no woman's fondness for children, nor was she interested in the apparently exciting anecdotes both her friends never seemed to run out of. At one point, giving a pause to her personal story, Prabhavati asked Mahadevi, 'So, when is your wedding? Or, are you still debating whether to wed or not to wed?'

'Soon,' Mahadevi said, blushing. 'It'll take place very soon, the like of which you would never have seen or heard?'

'Really! Come on, tell us, tell us who the boy is,' both the girls demanded.

Omkara Shetty and Lingamma, who walked a few steps behind the girls, looked at each other and sighed, as if to say: we don't know what is in her fate. Lingamma wanted to tell her husband about her strange conversation with Mahadevi that morning, but thought better of it.

The sun was on the hills and the greenery around felt like a soothing balm on a grieving heart. The family reached the royal street and saw crowds of people waiting for the arrival of King Kaushika. They had to wait for the royal cavalcade to pass, before proceeding to the temple.

Four soldiers on horses led the march, each carrying an orange-coloured triangular flag. Behind the soldiers came the king, riding a white stallion, smiling and waving to the crowd. A few paces behind the king rode his friend and confidante, Vasantaka, followed by a dozen armed soldiers on horses. As his eyes fell on Mahadevi, Kaushika gently tugged at the reins of his horse to stop. Her long and luxuriant hair was what attracted him at first. Vasantaka moved up from behind to the king's side and whispered, 'Majesty, people are watching you.' Mahadevi's eyes met Kaushika's for a moment and then she quickly looked away, feeling embarrassed. Prabhavati, gently, playfully pinched Mahadevi's arm and murmured, 'So this is the secret you were hiding from us, eh?' and Mahadevi's two friends giggled.

By evening the whole neighbourhood was agog with the news of the king's unabashed attraction to Mahadevi. And then Vasantaka came, along with four soldiers and six women carrying silver plates filled with silks and jewels and an assortment of fruits. The turn of events was so unexpected and sudden that Shetty did not know how to react, and Lingamma looked equally bewildered and lost. But Mahadevi, who had remained inside her room when Vasantaka arrived, was not surprised. She knew, she had had a premonition of the coming events.

'You really should be proud and happy for your daughter,' Vasantaka began. 'She'll be the queen of Uduthadi.'

Omkara Shetty looked confused and did not know what to say. How did this happen? He had no clue. It was all too sudden. He frowned, and then his face turned dark with a sense of foreboding. He began to sweat, his mouth went dry; but he had to respond, say something. Slowly, gathering courage, invoking the name of the Lord in his mind, he said, 'We are Shiva saranas. And we do not marry outside our community.'

Vasantaka did not expect Omkara Shetty to jump at the offer. He knew the saranas were too proud a lot and so he had expected some initial resistance. But Shetty's reply, delivered in a flat yet emphatic tone, sounded too arrogant. 'Don't be a fool,' Vasantaka said, with an edge to his voice. 'It's the king of the land who is seeking your daughter's hand.'

'Even if he is a King,' snapped Shetty.

Vasantaka clenched his jaws in controlled anger, but before he could warn Shetty of dire consequences if he declined the offer, Mahadevi rushed out of her room and stood by her father, her face flushed with rage.

'Brother,' she said sharply, 'I'm already married. Lord Chennamalikarjuna is my husband.'

Vasantaka had lowered his eyes when Mahadevi had come out. She was to be the king's wife and it would be bad manners to look straight in the face of the would-be queen of Uduthadi. But now he looked up, and saw her staring fearlessly at him. Her large, penetrating eyes paralysed him and he spoke no more.

'How could you come back empty-handed?' Kaushika exploded in anger at his friend. His mind was made up, he yelled. Come what may, Mahadevi would be his wife. 'Offer them anything, anything they want,' he cried desperately. 'All my wealth; even my palace. Tell them I'll accept all their demands and conditions. If they still refuse, threaten them. Tell them that punishment for their disobedience to the king will be death. They'll be hanged in public and all their relatives will be thrown into prison.' And finally, Kaushika warned his friend, 'Don't come back without Mahadevi. Break them to my will. I want her.'

Mahadevi took the matter into her own hands. Kaushika was quite capable of sending her parents to prison, even putting them to death. Kings turned beastly when their orders were disobeyed, when their desires were thwarted.

'God is cruel,' her father cried in anguish.

'We do not know the ways of God,' Mahadevi said. And she decided, 'What will happen will happen.'

She then met Guru Lingadeva and said to him, 'I don't want my parents to die and my people to suffer because of me. I'm ready to marry Kaushika.' Surprised and yet not wholly taken aback, Lingadeva said, 'You do not have to sacrifice your life for anybody, even for your parents. Kaushika cannot put us all into prison, much less kill us.'

Smiling wryly, Mahadevi replied, 'This is no sacrifice, Gurudeva. What is there to sacrifice when nothing belongs to me, including this bundle of flesh and bones which Kaushika desires.'

On hearing of Mahadevi's decision, Shetty ran to the matha, this time to beg the guru to intervene and stop Mahadevi.

'Sit down, Omkara,' said Lingadeva.

As Omkara squatted down, looking distraught and ready to cry, the guru said, 'It is only now that I understand why Mahadevi is doing this. She wants to free you and your wife and me from any blame. She wants the decision to be entirely hers so that whatever happens she would be responsible for it.'

'But this is madness! And all this to save our lives,' Shetty cried, choking on his words.

'Don't despair,' said the guru. 'Who knows, Mahadevi may be doing this to save Kaushika's life. Through her love and devotion, she might change Kaushika into a Shiva-bhakta.'

'No, no, no...' cried Shetty, tears running down his face. 'They say for a girl marriage is like a second birth, a second life, but this cruel marriage is no new birth but death.'

'No, Omkara, don't speak like that,' admonished the guru. 'I always have told you Mahadevi is different. It's a blessing that she's your daughter. And I really feel fortunate to have known her and taught her, though I cannot claim to be her guru.'

The following day, Omkara Shetty and Lingamma did not come out to see their daughter off, but almost the entire neighbourhood was out on the street, watching a cheerless Mahadevi come out and climb into the palanquin. Vasantaka was there, and soldiers on horses, giving a royal touch to the convoy. Of all Mahadevi's friends, only Prabhavati dared to go up to the palanquin to bid farewell to her friend. Mahadevi moved the silk curtain aside and tried to smile.

'You don't look happy, Mahadevi? Why?' asked the friend. 'Don't destroy the happiness that has come to you unasked. Only one in a million is as fortunate as you are.'

'Happiness is not what I seek, Prabha,' said Mahadevi gravely. 'You keep yourself happy and let me know when your child is born.' And then she leaned back, shutting her eyes to the world around.

At the palace, Kaushika never stopped smiling. 'Mahadevi, Mahadevi,' he kept chanting, and his face was a cup of overflowing joy. Mahadevi came clad in her dull grey sari and wore no jewels. She had refused to wear the silks and jewellery Kaushika had sent for her. Sacred ash smeared on her forehead, she came like an ascetic rather than a bride. But she came and that is all that mattered to Kaushika. He was prepared to accept anything and everything, as long as she agreed to be his wife. But he was least prepared when she said, 'No, not now. Not until you fulfil the conditions and not until we are ready for each other.'

Kaushika did not respond. Stunned, wide-eyed, he gazed at her peculiar beauty, at her thick lustrous tresses draped over her shoulders and back like unbounded passion, at her body that seemed to radiate sheer sensuality, despite her religious garb. He was only a minor king, but with a vaulting ambition to become the emperor of the whole of South. All that seemed trivial now before his burning passion to possess her, to have her as his queen.

Ignoring Kaushika's hungry look, Mahadevi continued in an even tone, as if she were giving instructions about the proper way to cook a good meal. 'Your friend must already have told you about my conditions to stay here,' she said. 'Still, I'll tell them once again and I want your honest answer.'

Coming out of his daze, Kaushika said, 'Anything you say, Mahadevi,' as if his words of assurance were good enough to win her heart.

'You should not come in the way of my devotion to Lord Shiva, my sadhana...' Mahadevi continued.

'Never,' Kaushika agreed too eagerly. 'You can go on with your pujas and rituals. You can even meet with your guru and visiting jangamas. I have no objection.'

'You should accept Lord Shiva.'

'Your God is my God, my dear,' Kaushika chuckled. 'But I need time. I'll be honest with you. I'm not used to worshipping your Lord Shiva with snakes around his neck, but I'll try. Just give me some time.'

'That is no bhakti. Devotion to God must come from the heart.'

'Yes, yes, I know. I'll change; I assure you, I'll change and you'll see it.'

In his late twenties, tall and well built, blessed with a sharp aquiline nose and large eyes, a thin moustache over his full lips, Kaushika was a handsome king even a princess would have felt proud to marry. Mahadevi now looked up and studied Kaushika, wondering not at his masculine frame and good looks, but if he was speaking the truth. Her large eyes bore into his and he felt a strange feeling invade his being, like a tidal wave against a ship.

'You should not touch me,' Mahadevi declared her third and final condition. 'And you should not force me to do anything against my wish and will. I'll not wed you, not now, not until we are ready for each other.'

Kaushika gave a short laugh, a gentle yet a jumpy laugh. 'Rest assured, Mahadevi,' he said. 'I'm a King, not an animal, or some street boy craving for your love. But remember one thing: I love you more than anything else in my life, more than even my life. I'll not touch you until you give me your consent and become my wife the proper way. I give you my word as King.'

'Your friend is our witness,' Mahadevi said, glancing sideways at Vasantaka, who stood at a distance, looking mystified. 'If you break your promise, I'll leave you. Now you may get my room ready for my stay.'

Kaushika could not believe his ears. He was ready for any sacrifice, ready even to kill, if necessary, to get Mahadevi. But he had not expected things would happen so soon, and that Mahadevi herself would willingly come to the palace. The conditions she had laid for her stay did not matter much. In fact, he did not take them seriously at all. Now that she was going to be there, it would be just a matter of time, he believed, before Mahadevi herself would run into his arms.

But, as days passed, the waiting game became unbearable. His desire for her reached a fever pitch. His body burned constantly, his limbs ached, his head felt heavy. He could not sleep, tossing about in his bed, his mind smouldering with a single thought: 'When will she be mine, when?'

'You must appear normal, Majesty,' Vasantaka warned him. 'You are a King; never forget that. She must come to you, and she will have to. Have patience, my King, appear normal, at least outwardly. Draw her into some interesting conversation, but don't lose your control.'

The advice only made Kaushika angry and restless. Still, he tried to be normal and pretended to be quite happy with things as they were. He watched her at her prayers and meditations and burned with desire. From time to time, when he managed to talk to her, he tried to talk about religious matters even though he had little interest in them, and he tried to look composed yet casual and laugh at silly nothings.

Almost all the time of the day and night, Mahadevi immersed herself in prayers, or spent whole days with the jangamas who passed through like flocks of birds. She refused to wear the royal costume, instead wearing only the simple cotton she had brought from home. She got the regal cot removed and slept on the floor. She ate her frugal meals from plantain leaves.

Kaushika bore it all patiently, telling himself: it's just a matter of time; she can't possibly go on like this for too long. But there was no sign of her ever changing and accepting Kaushika as her husband. She lived in the palace like an ascetic, and it seemed, she did it deliberately to insult him, to mock at his kingly power and lifestyle. One day, Kaushika got so disgusted and angry at waiting that he almost decided to throw her parents into prison if she did not give in and wed him right away.

'These methods will not work,' Vasantaka chided him. 'She'll never be yours if you do that.'

But Kaushika could not go on burning with desire and not being able to fulfil it. No, he decided, he would not wait for her to come to him. He had given her enough time. The only way he could make her his wife was to either put her parents behind bars, forcing her to submit to him, or take her even if it was by force. Only then would she bend and change and become his. She would have no choice.

'Nothing is obvious,' protested Bahurupi. 'Every bit of reality is intertwined with hundred other realities in hundred mysterious ways. What we think as obvious is only a deception of the mind!'

'You protest too much, man. Just stand there and tell the story,' said Nage.

'There are too many misgivings,' confessed Bahurupi.

'Every story is a paradox, my friend,' said Nage, screwing up his face in mock annoyance. 'You may look at it from several perspectives and still be troubled by a sense of doubt and dissatisfaction. Just go ahead and tell the story the way you feel deeply about it and let people decide for themselves what it means. In any case, that's what always happens, people take what they want and they are not wrong. Whether it's for good or for bad, that's how things always have been.

'Now, about Mahadevi and your misgivings about her. I know you are not on sure ground while telling her story. There are too many missing links, too many gaps, you complain. But, come on, brother, that's true of everybody's story. Every story is incomplete and splintered. So, about Mahadevi, let's just say she is different, or, made differently! Why shouldn't she be? Why should she be like your wife or other so-called normal, menstruating women of the kind you seemed to have known too many? What is 'normal', after all, Bahurupi? Strange are the ways of maya, as you keep saying. Now, enough of this needless chatter. No more explanations, no more philosophy. Let's stick to the story.'

And for a change, Nage told three stories to the storyteller.

'Listen, Bahurupi. Tapasya is a means to immortality and so is sex. Shiva combines both, for he is the paradox, and he is life. When he is into tapas without pause, his tapasic heat begins to burn and destroy the world. But that cannot be, so, Kama, the love god, intervenes and flings his flower-tipped arrow of desire at Shiva. Disturbed, Shiva opens his eyes and wonders: "How can I desire to make love to Parvati? How can I be excited by passion while I am in tapas? What is happening?" It is of course inevitable; it is natural. The creative process has to begin, the world cannot be allowed to shrivel up and come to a standstill. If Shiva's desire creates the world, his tapasya destroys it. The cycle of creation and destruction must go on and it goes on endlessly. But a point comes and it comes rarely when Shiva, tired of this endless process, absorbs Parvati into his body and realizes he is both, Parvati and Shiva, both feminine and masculine, Prakriti and Purusha. For the one to whom this happens is neither completely a male nor a female, and yet he combines both qualities and he is Shiva the ardhanaraishwara. For such a one there is no birth and no death, only the rhythm of the movement of life changes in tune with the cosmic order. Do you understand what that is? If you didn't, then, ask Allama when you meet him next.

'Now, listen closely to the story of Indra, the King of Heavens. He had many wives, and several mistresses, too, all as beautiful as beauty can be. Still, he never felt happy or fulfilled. Such is the nature of sexual desire: you'll never be satisfied, when the genital impulse travels up and lodges itself as desire in the mind! You may abstain from sex or you may indulge yourself in sex to extirpate your sexuality. It doesn't help. You may, of course, restrain yourself from overindulgence. Self-restraint may be a trick, an art to limit the unlimited, so that you do not fall into the circle of desire and spin round and round without arriving at a sense of fulfilment; though, I must say, even that doesn't help.

'But Indra was a king, a god, and both kings and gods are such ignorant fools. So, Indra, despite having heavenly women at his beck and call, fell madly in love with Ahalya, the wife of Maharshi Gautama. He worked himself up into such a fever pitch of desire that he wanted to possess her by fair means or foul. So, one day, when in the early hours Gautama had gone to the river for his ablutions, Indra took the form of the rishi, entered the cottage and made love to Ahalya. But, as fate would have it, just as he was coming out of the cottage, Gautama returned. Instantly he knew what had passed. Enraged, Gautama cursed Indra: "Let your whole body bear a thousand vulva-shaped marks, and let the whole world see and laugh and wonder and reflect upon your fate."

'And poor King Indra became a laughing stock of the whole world,' quipped Bahurupi, with a good laugh. 'But, tell me, was it really a curse or a joke?'

'Both,' said Nage. 'For the one who suffers, it is a curse. For others, it is a joke. Any public display of sex becomes at once obscene and amusing, just as impropriety becomes a folly and a vice, especially when gods and kings and holy men indulge in it. There is also disgust and awakening into knowledge. Indra's fall, you may say, also paves the way to knowledge and wisdom.'

'You club too many ideas and confuse me,' protested Bahurupi. 'Why don't you simply say pride comes before the fall?'

'It is not entirely true in the case of Indra. He was a buffoon,' said Nage, giggling, gathering his hair in a bunch and tossing it over his shoulder. 'But what you say is quite true in the case of King Mahishasura. Aham, egoism, is the evil, is the sin, for it alienates you from the life around you and the world, and you fall into illusion. That is dangerous and self-destructive.

'But that is how Mahishasura brought upon himself his own destruction. Yes, power and pride come before the fall. Gloating over his sway over the three worlds, Mahishasura's eye fell on Devi. I am all-powerful and invincible, and I am the overlord of the universe. Everything belongs to me, except this beautiful woman. I'll take her and fulfil my desire, Mahishasura said to himself, roaring with laughter, like a terrible rakshasa he was. And he sent Devi a message asking her to become his wife. Enraged by his inexcusable impropriety, Devi replied that she would become his wife only if he defeats her in a battle. Devi's challenge only made Mahishasura's fascination for her and his desire to possess her multiply a hundredfold.

Cackling and twirling his huge moustache, he entered the battlefield, carrying his deadly weapons and accompanied by his terrifying army of soldiers. And there she stood, in the middle of the battlefield, the goddess: naked, fire leaping from her eyes, carrying a blazing sword in one hand and a lethal spear in the other. Mahishasura shivered at the fiery form of the goddess and that very instant his desire for her evaporated, replaced by a terrible fear. Devi began a wild tandava of death, and in no time, in swift, rhythmic movement, she cut to pieces the demon soldiers. Mahishasura bolted, fearing for his life. Devi chased him, her sword drenched with blood. To escape from her wrath, Mahishasura took the form of a wild buffalo, but the raging goddess swiftly jumped on the animal's back and rode it until he could move no more. Then Devi plunged her pointed spear into the buffalo's ear and the greedy King fell dead.'

Bahurupi gave a long sigh. 'So what are you trying to say?'

'I'm not saying anything,' said Nage. 'I'm only telling you stories.'

'Yes, they are very interesting, quite enlightening, too. But what are you saying through this one?'

'I think the story speaks for itself. Still, if you insist and if I must explain, I would say Devi is Mahishasura's destiny. And Shiva is Devi's destiny. Even after killing the demon, Devi's macabre dance of death did not cease. The gods feared that if Devi did not stop, the terrific heat she generated would burn up the world, and so they ran to Shiva and pleaded with him to intervene. Shiva realized that the only way Devi could be made quiet was to appease her wrath. So, Shiva surrendered, and, through him, the powers of the world surrendered to Devi. He lay down on his back and let Devi dance over him. Dancing upon Shiva's breast, Devi grew shy and calm and came to rest in the heart of the Lord.'

Words give substance and power to thoughts. King Kaushika did not realize that to break his word given to Mahadevi was to change the course of his life and Mahadevi's as well. But then he was helpless, as helpless as the many Indras of many cycles of time, in the presence of a female body. Perhaps more helpless and hopeless than the rishis of yore who, coming out of their long and fierce tapas, fell madly in love with the first woman they happened to lay their eyes on. Kaushika was of course no believer in chastity, nor was he a seeker of God.

Freshly bathed, clad in her sari, her long and thick hair still wet, her forehead smeared with holy ash, eyes shut and the sacred linga cupped in her raised left palm, Mahadevi sat in meditation. Kaushika had promised not to disturb her while she was into her sacred hour. He had kept his word all these days. But today, with his patience at an end and his desire unleashed, he could not resist breaking his resolution and his word. The sight of Mahadevi's body, accentuated by the wet sari sticking to her skin, inflamed his mind and body. Breathing heavily, like an animal in heat, in three quick strides he crossed the room and tried to take her by force.

Mahadevi's eyes flew open and her whole body burned in sudden rage. Pushing him away, she leapt to her feet, with fire in her eyes. Kaushika fell back, the hem of her sari twisted between his trembling fingers.

With one firm tug, Mahadevi loosened the sari at her waist and naked she stood, like a furious sun in a cloudless sky.

'This is what you want, what you lust for, this body, this bag of flesh and bones,' she cried. 'Look, King Kaushika, open your eyes wide and look, and take this body if you can.'

Kaushika could not look at her, for it was like looking at the sudden dawn of a million suns. His body turned stiff, and his mind blank. He lay sprawled on the floor, with the bare sari lying by his side in a heap.

He had broken his promise, broken the last condition that had been laid upon him if he wanted her to live with him. Now, with the bond between them broken, like a bird at last freed from her cage, Mahadevi turned and walked away and out of Kaushika's life, from her hitherto incarcerated life as the would-be-queen in the palace, from her past that now seemed a heap of mere ash. She strode through and out of the corridors of the palace, hearing and not hearing the cries and pleas of her maids, past the guards who stood aghast, her breasts bouncing with pride, her eyes aglow with the new-found joy and wonder.

Like a snake that sheds its old skin, Mahadevi shed her needless modesty and cumbersome sari. Like Shiva, who walked naked through the Pine Forest, his skin burning and shining like burnished gold, Mahadevi, giving a strange twist to the tale, sky-clad, walked past the civilized world, in quest of Shiva, whom she called Lord Chennamalikarjuna, her Lord White as Jasmine.

> *Take these husbands who die and decay,*
> *feed them to your kitchen fires.*
> *The one with no name, no form,*
> *no death, no origins,*
> *Lord Chennamalikarjuna*
> *is my husband.*

Naked as she was born, her untied hair curling and swaying like a million tiny serpents over her body, she strode up the royal street and her every step resonated through Uduthadi like a thunderclap. It was a spectacle the likes of which they had never witnessed before. While some laughed and jeered and hooted at her, many were stunned by the naked figure and her long hair now streaming out on the wind like a comet; and they felt, with a tremble in their heart, that it was a sign of some great change to come and their lives wouldn't be the same again.

Mahadevi went straight to the matha. Soon, Omkara Shetty and Lingamma came running there and cried together, 'What happened, Mahadevi? What happened? What have you done, my child?'

Guru Lingadeva said, 'Mahadevi, this will not help. The world will not understand you. Take this cloth and cover yourself.'

'Are you afraid of yourself, Gurudeva?' Mahadevi asked bluntly.

'I'm afraid for you,' said the guru, avoiding her eyes. 'Do not mistake me. But the world is not yet ready.'

'Come home, Mahadevi,' the parents cried together. 'Whatever has happened has happened. We are with you. Please come home, this is too embarrassing.'

A strange smile appeared on Mahadevi's face. She looked calm. And, straight as an arrow, she said, 'I'm finished with this world of yours. I came here only to say farewell. From now on, nothing exists for me but my Lord Chennamalikarjuna.'

'Where will you go, my child, where?' cried Lingamma.

'Don't you know, mother?' Mahadevi asked, smiling wearily and looking into her mother's eyes. 'Where else but to Kalyana, the abode of Shiva-bhaktas! There I'll meet Brother Basava and Prabhu Allama. Kalyana will be my home, and Kadali my destiny.'

Anna Basava

There is something about Basavanna that is difficult to explain. He was not tall or handsome, nor was he what you would call charismatic. He was of average height with a cleft chin and simple looks, and walked with a little stoop, as if burdened with the weight of the sorrows of the world, or perhaps it was a physical sign of his humility. 'There is none younger than me,' he would say, deeply embarrassed when every time someone praised him too highly. What drew people to him were his tender smile and sweet words and sad face. If his generous, tender smile made people want to touch him, fall at his feet and feel assured that everything would be fine in his saintly presence; his sad, melancholic face made people feel connected and want to hug him and weep over his shoulder, forgetting all their conflicts and suffering and come upon that lightness of being. He was like a river that nourished parched earth, giving birth to new life, a new beginning, they said.

From early morning till evening, the Brahmin neighbourhood in Bagevadi resounded with Vedic chanting, devotional songs and Sanskrit learning. Basava's father, Madiraja, was a Vedic scholar and the head of the Brahmin community of that town. By the time Basava was seven, he was quite conversant with Sanskrit and could chant the Vedas with perfect intonation. Despite such religious upbringing, or because of it, Basava grew to be a rebel, but in a quiet sort of way. He hardly ever openly and aggressively opposed his elders and teachers, yet seldom did he follow their orders.

At the age of eight, however, with much reluctance and resentment, he underwent the *upanayana*, the sacred thread ceremony.

'Why should I wear this long thread?' he asked his father.

'We are Brahmins and it is our tradition. Unless you go through this sacred ceremony you will not be entitled to be called a Brahmin,' said the father.

'Why don't other boys wear this?' Basava persisted.

The other boys were not Brahmins, his father said. They belonged to the caste lower than that of a Brahmin, that their customs and rituals were different.

The young Basava saw no fundamental difference between him and the other boys and he was sharp enough to sense that his father's answers were only variations of the answers he had given to his other trying questions on different occasions. The answers always revolved around the notion of Brahminhood, and the sacred tradition, handed down from generation to generation, and it was their bounden duty to follow these ancient, sacred decrees. This is what the sacred scriptures say and what the gods wish, his father would assert. But, gradually, something in Basava began to revolt against such beliefs and practices, though he could not clearly tell what he was against.

Not wanting to hurt his parents, he went through the motions of the sacred thread ceremony. And then, a year later, as an act of defiance, he grew long hair and insisted on wearing earrings.

'This is the practice of our ancestors and I cannot go against it,' he told his shocked teacher.

'Don't act like a low-caste scoundrel,' his father scolded him. 'Brahmins don't wear their hair long.'

Basava silenced him, saying, 'Shiva came in my dream and commanded me to wear earrings and grow my hair long.'

Four years later, with the support of his eccentric uncle, who was much feared by the community for his subversive reading of the scriptures and his short temper, Basava left Bagevadi to join the matha at Kappadisangama. Under the guidance of Guru Ishanya, Basava studied the Vedas, the Agamas, the non-Vedic texts, and was introduced to Kashmiri Shaivism and the Shaivism of the Nayanaras. It was here at Kappadisangama, exposed to different spiritual discourses and through rigorous sadhana, Basava came upon his calling and became a spiritual radical.

On the day he heard about the untimely death of his parents, he tore off his sacred thread and went for a dip in Kappadisangama, where the rivers Krishna and Malaprabha merged. Bare-bodied, water dripping from his hair, just as he came up the banks, he was surprised to see his Guru.

'Basava,' cried Guru Ishanya, who had followed him there. 'What are you up to? Don't try to impress and confound me by talking about your dreams and visions. Speak the truth.'

'I always speak the truth,' swore Basava. 'What I see are not mere dreams but a tremendous reality, more real than what I see and experience of this world.' He held out the linga wrapped in a piece of ochre cloth, with a string tied at two ends. As the guru watched him in bewilderment, Basava, chanting the name of his God, wore the linga around his neck.

Intrigued, the guru asked, 'So you don't need a formal initiation by a guru?'

'I need your blessings,' said Basava and knelt before the guru. The guru laid his hand on Basava's head and said, 'Now get up and live your new life. Let Lord Shiva be your guide and light. Do not look back.'

Basava never looked back.

Three years later, one summer day, as the evening descended on Kappadisangama like a dream and the sun coloured the united rivers in gold, with the linga held in his palm at the eye-level, Basava stepped into the Sangama, the meeting place of the rivers, and made a promise to himself:

'There is no God other than Lord Shiva. I'll never sway from my path, never rest until I reach my goal, until I become one with Him, who is everywhere and in everything, who is the source and ground of all existence. There is none high or low; all are one. I shall be the dust of dust under Your feet and I shall have no life of my own. All is Yours.'

And then he scooped the sacred water in his cupped palms and chanted:

> I do not know anything like time-beats and metre,
> nor the arithmetic of strings and drums;
> I do not know the count of iamb and dactyl.
> My lord of the meeting rivers,
> as nothing will hurt You
> I'll sing as I love, and
> live as You command.

For two years, Basava toured the country, meeting yogis and pandits, truth-seekers and worldly men, fools and artists, gamblers and harlots, bhaktas and drunkards. And he saw, from up close, life so bewilderingly varied and complex that his mind went numb. But he told himself, 'Lord, this is your maya. You manifest through a million faces and tongues, through a million forms and names. I shall not be trapped. I see only Thee behind these apparent distinctions, these different forms and names. Lord, I know you are beyond every name and form.'

He saw the wealthy swell with pride and scholars grin with arrogance and he felt sad. He saw the face of humility and the wretchedness of the poor and the low caste and grew angry. He saw sanyasis eat like gluttons and yogis wasting away in their tapas. At a village square, he heard about Allama Prabhu and yearned to meet him, but without success. In every village people said that Allama had passed through their place but none could tell him where he could be found.

During this journey, he composed vachanas, forty-six of them. He went to the celebration of a festival and saw a garlanded, sacrificial lamb, bleating away happily. Moved by the innocent animal and deeply disturbed by the inhuman ritual of animal sacrifice, he wrote:

> *The sacrificial lamb brought for the festival*
> *ate up the green leaf brought for the decorations.*
> *Not knowing a thing about the kill,*
> *it wants only to fill its belly:*
> *born that day, to die that day.*
> *But tell me:*
> *Did the killers survive?*

The orthodox Brahmins everywhere appeared to be deceiving and impervious to the changes around them. Though they belonged to different sects, they all seemed the same to him, manipulating the Vedas and Shastras to give themselves both social and religious authority over society and people. They had lost the spirit of inquiry and truth and clung to dead words and rituals.

> *They feed the fire as a god.*
> *When the fire goes wild and burns the house,*
> *they forget their worship and scold their fire.*
> *They splash on it the water of the gutter,*
> *the dust of the street,*
> *beat their breasts and call the crowd.*

Returning to Kappadisangama, he went directly to his uncle's house and said, 'It seems I haven't eaten a good meal for ages.' He ate as much as he could and slept for eighteen hours. The next day, he met Guru Ishanya at the matha.

The guru asked, 'So, how was your journey?'

The long journey that had brought him in contact with people from all walks of life had enlarged his vision and deepened his spiritual search, and he had matured into a fine poet. But he felt incomplete and a deep sorrow burned in him like ague. Shaking his head and with a heavy heart, he replied, rather cryptically,

> *I went to fornicate,*
> *but all I got was counterfeit.*
> *I went behind a ruined wall,*
> *but scorpions stung me.*
> *The guard who heard my screams*
> *just peeled off my clothes.*
> *I went home in shame,*
> *my husband raised weals on my back.*
> *All the rest, the king took for his fines.*

'Good for you!' said Ishanya, giggling, which surprised Basava. And then the guru asked, bluntly, 'So what do you want to do now?'

'I don't know,' replied Basava.

'That is a good state to be in,' commented Ishanya, it seemed playfully, and left his one-time disciple to his own devices.

Basava did not really know what he should do next. He had gone out searching for answers and come back feeling empty and wretched. Indeed it was like the woman who had sought pleasure outside marriage only to return home shamed, bruised and disillusioned. That evening, at the sangama, when birds flew in hordes over the river bank to their nests, a soft breeze came out the waters and caressed his now shaven, pale face, and the waters murmured like soft lullabies, raising his eyes to the skies, Basava prayed:

> *Shiva, you have no mercy,*
> *you have no heart.*
> *Why did you bring me to birth,*
> *wretch in this world,*
> *exile from the other?*
> *Tell me, Lord,*
> *don't you have one more little plant*
> *made just for me?*

A week later came the call from Bijjala. Basava's uncle, Baladeva, who was an official in Bijjala's court, had recommended his name for a position. And the king asked Basava to join his court as his chief officer of accounts. But Basava was not sure if he should accept the offer. His sister, Nagakka, said that he should.

'See it as another journey you need to take,' Guru Ishanya said. 'Who knows, Kudalasangamadeva may have something in it for you. Moreover, you wouldn't want to disappoint your uncle and disobey a king's order.'

Basava complied, but not without misgivings. A year later, after Bijjala established himself, though controversially, as King of the Chalukya Empire, Basava, now promoted to the rank of a minister in charge of the treasury, went to work and live at Kalyana.

Within a few days of arriving at Kalyana, Basava wanted to quit his post and return to Kappadisangama. Unlike his previous job at Mangalvada, the job at the treasury was quite demanding and he did not quite feel equal to the task, although the king was quite responsive and supportive. He could deal with the fact that the staff at the treasury was not entirely above suspicion. He was not the one who would turn away from facing such problems and challenges of life. His greatest fear and anxiety, however, was the disruption of his spiritual pursuit and undivided devotion to his Lord. And when he went to the lake to take a boat back to Kappadisangama, as fate would have it, the boatman happened to be Chowdayya, the same bearded one who had ferried him across Tripuranthaka Lake to Kalyana. Basava had taken an instant liking to the man. Seeing him again he talked freely about his dilemma, and why he yearned to go back to Kappadisangama.

'I have seen the poor hunger for food,' the boatman said, 'but once their bellies are filled, they begin to crave for clothes and fancy things; once that craving too is satisfied, they desire for a woman and family life; and once they get married, children appear in the family and they find their worries multiply a hundredfold and they do not know how to cope with them. And I have seen the rich and the powerful, too, who never seem to find satisfaction with what they have and they too hanker after more wealth and power only to end up equally confused, lost and unhappy. But I have never seen someone so worried about one's God.'

'Brother Chowdayya,' Basava smiled and opened his heart to him. 'Shiva is my path, my goal, my life, the very breath of my existence!'

'I can see that you are a great devotee of Lord Shiva. You are a blessed man! What then is your problem?' asked Chowdayya.

'I'm afraid that my work at the treasury would come in the way of my total devotion to the Lord. So I would rather leave the job and go back than suffer this separation.'

'I do understand your anxiety, Basava,' Chowdayya said, smiling through his great beard. 'But isn't it possible that this is what the Lord wants you to do and the reason why he has sent you to Kalyana? Work cannot take us away from God, but only closer to Him. Don't you think so?'

Basava nodded, pondering over Chowdayya's words, and Chowdayya continued, 'I see a peculiar glow on your face. Over these years I must have ferried thousands across the lake, but I haven't seen anyone like you in my entire life. Perhaps you are the one Kalyana has been waiting for. You are the guru we have been waiting for so long. Take us with you, Basava. Lead us to the truth. We'll be blessed to have you as our Guru.'

Kalyana was not only the centre of political power and of trade and commerce, but it was a religious centre as well. The rich merchants lived in the city and so did the religious leaders of various sects. There were monstries of Jains, Shaivites, Vaishnavites and Kalamukhas, and many temples, large and small, most of them under the stronghold of the priestly class and the adherents of Pashupath Shaivism. Amidst these religious sects came a new kind of Shiva bhaktas and they grew thick and fast like tall grass across the land.

'Tell me, Lord, don't you have one more little plant just for me?' Basava had asked of Lord Sangameshvara at Kappadisangama. At Kalyana, the little plant that Basava planted grew into a gigantic tree. Cutting across caste and community, people flocked around Basava like bees, and Kalyana grew like a colossal beehive. It was a miracle and at the centre of this miracle shone Basava, like a bright star, and people could not take their eyes off him, nor stop listening to his words. 'But I am nothing,' Basava warned them, and all through he kept telling himself that he was not the doer but Shiva was, that he was only a channel, a medium for the divine force.

Boatmen, washermen, watermen, tanners, cobblers, tailors, barbers, shepherds, labourers, basket weavers, fishermen, toddy sellers and peasants were in the forefront of this army of resurgent Shaivism. And among them sprang poets, both men and women, of great spiritual depth and understanding. And each one brought his or her unique insights and idiom into the rich repertoire of vachanas. There were of course some whose vachanas were prosaic and poor imitation of Basavanna's inimitable vachanas. However, there were many saranas who tread their own path, whose vachanas were fleshed out from the depth of their experience. If some were direct and even candid to a fault, some were profound, complex and mystical. Through irony, paradox, abuse, assertion, and by drawing images from their vocation and every day experiences, they spoke of their perception of things, about pretensions and false devotion, the absurdity of orthodoxy, and false consciousness. Their work, their vocation, whether it was carrying water, cooking, cow-herding, ferrying people across lakes and rivers, cobbling sandals, or washing clothes—what they called *kayaka*—was no different from the act of worshipping Shiva. And their sense of wonder at the ways of the world and the mystery of Shiva sometimes took the form of intense inquiry:

> *What is shame for a dumb woman? ...*
>
> *O Lord, what can you say of one who beats himself and then complains of pain? ...*
>
> *When the field goes naked, what can you cover it with? ...*
>
> *After discarding your clothes, why should you guard someone else's? ...*
>
> *What is the caste of atma? ...*
>
> *Can you string bubbles of water together? ...*
>
> *After giving up everything, what is town and what forest? ...*

The women poets did not mince words when they critiqued social evils, man-made values and religious superstitions. Their vachanas were fiery and like arrows they often hit the target with great effect:

> *Lord, I cannot trust these tonsured men in rags carrying pitchers, I don't need guru linga, jangama, holy water and what have you...*
>
> *...reject these husbands, if you have to be one with Shiva...*
>
> *...shoo away these scholars, they all are hollow like empty pots...*
>
> *The discourses of Vedic scholars are mere gossip in a fair, their narratives a fool's seminar...*
>
> *...hoping for Kailasa through devotion is like expecting wages for your labour...*
>
> *Woman is not an illusion but an aspect of God...*
>
> *Union with Linga is like camphor in fire, like fragrance in the air...*

Basava was in the middle of this revolution, both as its cause and as its effect. Yet, despite his deep involvement, sometimes he would find himself vacillating, swinging between disgust and euphoria, between demands of absolute renunciation and creative engagement with society.

> *Like a monkey on a tree,*
> *it leaps from branch to branch:*
> *how can I trust this burning thing,*
> *this heart?*
> *It will not let me go to my Lord,*
> *O Kudalasangamadeva.*

Or, sometimes growing desperate, he would call out,

> *Cripple me, Lord,*
> *that I may not go here and there.*

*Blind me, Lord,
that I may not look at this and that.
Deafen me, Lord,
that I may not hear anything else...*

Basava knew that just as the tree is in the seed, all conflict and suffering is in the asking, yet, he could not help but ask, pray; there was no other way. The path of knowledge, of tapasya, was not for him. His was the path of bhakti, and applicable to other saranas too, to negotiate the world of this painful duality, in order to reach the shore of unity, the Infinite absolute.

Six years passed, like a gratifying dream. The little plant he had planted and nourished with great care, grew beyond his imagination. It stemmed the religious rot, and offered a new meaning and purpose to the millions of saranas. But he was not at peace. For, however much he justified the way of bhakti, the deep urge in him to take to the path of renunciation never left him. And then things began to happen that tied him further down to the world he so much wanted to renounce, things that would not, in his own words, 'let me go to my Lord'.

One summer evening, while serving supper to Basava, Nagakka said, 'Brother, do you remember the day you left Kappadisangama?'

Basava paused. 'It was raining heavily. But your son's crying was deafening; he wouldn't let me leave.' He smiled, thinking of the near commotion little Chenna Basava had created that evening.

'I'm glad I decided to come to you. I have found my refuge.'

'Sister,' said Basava, looking up into her eyes. 'Shiva is our refuge.'

Nagakka now squatted down on the floor in front of Basava. Basava paused again and looked up. Nagakka smiled and it seemed to him that he had never seen her smile that way, like a shy little girl.

'Basava,' Nagakka said, 'you need a companion, you need a woman in your life. Get married.'

Basava was certainly not planning to lead a celibate's life. He had discouraged celibacy among his followers; suppression of sexual instinct would not take a sarana anywhere closer to truth and God than punishing one's body by standing on one leg to please God. This physical and mortal world is but the maker's mint, and a spiritual seeker has to live intelligently and with undivided devotion to God. And, asserting the spiritual significance and value of creative engagement with life, Basava would declare: 'Those who earn merit here, earn also there, and those who earn not here, earn not there either.'

And yet, till now he had not thought of his marriage, though he had encouraged and even presided over the marriages of several saranas.

'I have seen a girl,' the sister persisted, 'and she'll suit you in every way.'

'But, sister,' Basava said, face flushed and smiling awkwardly, yet unassuming and humble as always, 'will I be a suitable man for her?'

'Why don't you ask Ganga yourself?' his sister said, laughing.

The fair-skinned, fish-eyed daughter of his uncle Baladeva was not unknown to Basava. He had seen her at home with Nagakka on a few occasions and had taken a liking to her. He certainly needed a partner in life and she could be the one. Things had happened in his life without his having to make a conscious decision. And it happened again, without his having to exert his will. He married Ganga.

As fate would have it, she was not to be his only wife. A second proposal came from the king himself and he could not bring himself to decline the offer. He married King Bijjala's foster-sister, Neela. But a year into the marriage, he could not help feeling it was all bondage and yearned to free himself from the fetters of all relationships. At times, overcome with a sense of extreme disgust, he would lament, 'My life is like that of a dog licking a sword's sharp edge for ghee. O Lord, out of thy mercy rid me of this doggish life...O, like a beast fallen into a bog of greed, lust, sloth, lies, roguery and fraud, anger and meanness and untruth, I gasp this way and that...O Lord, when, when will I be free of this samsara and taste that supreme happiness untouched by sorrow?'

As the years rolled by, the sect grew from strength to greater strength, like the great Banyan tree, sending its aerial roots deep into the earth. The *Mahamane*, the Great Mansion, which at first Basava had thought was too big and extravagant for his needs, was now quite small for his rapidly growing family of saranas. Additional buildings had to be put up to accommodate visitors and jangamas, to hold meeting of Shiva-bhaktas, and to feed the saranas. Feeding the devotees, *Dasoha*, became a regular feature, for 'they are the face and mouth of the Lord, as the root below is the mouth of a tree'.

Devotees of Shiva and spiritual seekers of various persuasions came from even far-flung places like Kashmir, Gujarat, Saurashtra, Andhra and Kerala. They came to meet and deliberate over spiritual matters with Basava and they were overwhelmed by his depth of understanding and his caring hospitality. He became their Anna, elder brother, and around him grew the vibrant community of saranas, challenging the orthodoxy of Vedic Brahmins and rejecting traditional gender discrimination and Varnashrama dharma. These saranas saw themselves as the true, courageous devotees of Shiva.

The new faith also rejected other non-Brahminical belief systems and practices as irrelevant, immature and misleading. They rejected not only 'higher Gods' such as Lord Vishnu but also 'lower gods' and deities worshipped by the lower castes and tribals. Basava condemned animal sacrifice and other inhuman rituals practised by the lower castes. Indulgence in sex as a way to God and other extreme form of religious observances of certain religious sects were viewed with distaste and suspicion. They found Jain beliefs and practices too problematic and contrary to their view of life. The Jain's practice of abnegation and extreme asceticism was considered quite unnecessary and even dangerous. More importantly, in Jainism, there was no notion of God, no bhakti, and therefore, no relationship with God. 'Without bhakti do what you will; it'll be like washing a toddy-pot from outside,' declared Basava.

Bhakti was supreme. Bhakti was the mantra, the way and the goal. Sometimes the vigour and passion with which these saranas took to their beliefs and practices bordered on fanaticism. And there indeed was an element of militancy in the defence of their faith. It was sacrilegious to worship any form or symbol of God other than the linga. There was no caste discrimination amongst the Shiva-bhaktas, and to show their solidarity, it was essential for them to dine together like blood relatives. Dasoha, sharing food together, was one of the cardinal principles of the faith. Regard or respect towards each other was of paramount importance. And a sarana was called upon to conduct himself as if he was the youngest of the lot. Such humility between saranas was a great virtue, but not when a sarana was abused or ill-treated by others.

These new soldiers of Shiva were both messianic and militant in their approach and character. However, they were also extremely self-critical in their practice. Essentially their main battle, rather, their basic struggle, was not so much with other faiths and ideologies as with each other and within themselves. The obstacles to God-realization, or attainment of oneness with the Infinite Absolute, lay not outside, but within the heart and mind of the bhakta.

> *The rich will make temples for Shiva.*
> *What shall I, a poor man, do?*
> *My legs are pillars, the body the shrine,*
> *the head a cupola of gold.*
> *Listen, O Kudalasangamadeva,*
> *things standing shall fall,*
> *but the moving ever shall stay.*

This vachana of Basava succinctly summarized the central concern of the new cult of Shiva. It was at once a critique and the way out of the Vedic religion, and a call to return to *anubhaava*, the unmediated experience or vision of the Infinite Absolute.

The movement, however, was not without discord and differences, not without dispute and dissent from within, and not without corruption and chicanery. From time to time the movement swung from the profound to the ridiculous. Sometimes the practice of wearing the ishtalinga on the body went to extreme levels. They called it 'ishtalinga', 'dear linga', as opposed to 'sthavara linga', 'the fixed linga' installed and established in temples. Saranas wrapped the ishtalinga in a piece of cloth or set it in a small casket and wore it round their neck in such a way that it rested on their chest. Twice a day the devotee would take it out, hold it in his palm and worship. There were instances of saranas committing suicide when they happened to lose their ishtalinga.

Overenthusiastic saranas cast aspersions on the beliefs and practices of other faiths and poked fun at other symbols of god. Killing of a Brahmin, who was looked upon as the custodian of Vedic beliefs and values, was condemned by the tradition as the most heinous crime that demanded the severest punishment of the perpetrator. To a sarana, however, the Brahmin was an insufferable rival. Aggressive saranas did not think twice before thrashing Brahmins who dared to challenge them and insult Lord Shiva. Indeed, there were instances when such quarrels reached extreme levels, resulting in the killing of Brahmins.

Dasoha, the practice of sharing of food without caste discrimination, often floundered, given the deep-rooted caste prejudices. Not all jangamas would gladly share or accept food from saranas who originally came from low-castes. The 'high' and 'low' caste sensibility persisted in subtle ways, despite the avowed philosophy of absolute equality among the saranas. Temple worship could not be given up completely, nor meat eating by the low-caste converts. Basava viewed these deviations from the declared path sympathetically, for he knew the age-old practices would not be given up so easily. But, unlike Basava, Chenna Basava viewed these deviations as sacrilege, betrayal of faith. And at every sign of deviation from the path, he would warn, 'If you cannot give up liquor, meat and hemp, if you cannot stop worshipping gods and goddesses other than our Lord Shiva, and if you do not sever friendship with those who are not saranas, you may leave the path and go your way.'

The adherents of Pashupath Shaivism and Vaishnaivism, not to speak of the business class, landlords and those who belonged to the higher echelons of the government, were both alarmed and outraged at this high tide of radical religiosity sweeping across their society. Basava had cut into their social and religious authority and made them look like a self-centered, wicked lot. One-time shudras, the menial class, and even ati-shudras, the untouchables, who would cringe and crouch and bend over double with trembling reverence before them, now walked with their heads held high and looked fearlessly into their eyes. And women, who would cover their heads while speaking to men and who hardly stirred out of homes, now strutted about freely in public places, clad proudly in ochre saris, their foreheads smeared with holy ash. The ancient social order was in danger.

'This cannot be allowed. We have to stop this madness,' the orthodox Brahmins and those from the powerful upper castes growled in frustration and took the matter to King Bijjala. But Bijjala held Basava in high esteem for his good work, and was in awe of his extraordinary knowledge.

'You are making allegations against my minister, who is also related to me as my brother-in-law.' Bijjala warned, when the gang of Shastris and Dikshits and Damodaras, led by Mancharasa, went with their complaint against Basava.

Manacharasa, a short, corpulent man, a former senior official at the treasury who had lost the minister's post to Basava, said, 'Forgive me, Your Majesty, I wouldn't have dared to bring them before you if I hadn't found these allegations to be true.'

Shastri, his broad forehead marked with thick-red nama, signifying his sect, stood up in his shining silk robes, bowed his head thrice, and said, 'Your Majesty, you are our law-giver and protector. You are our ultimate authority and our refuge. Basavanna cannot be allowed to question your authority and subvert our ancient sacred laws and tradition. People have begun to believe that Basavanna is God, far above the authority of our sacred scriptures, far above the authority of even the king. He and his followers have become a real danger not only to our sacred tradition, but to your power as well.'

Dikshit, a man of vast wealth and power, was quite a familiar figure in the king's court. When his turn came, smiling from ear to ear, he said, 'I have met Basava and know him well. I have no doubt in my mind that, in the name of social service and spiritual sadhanas, Basava is raising an army. And he has gathered enormous wealth around him which he uses generously to lure people into his sect. Poor people, with no proper shelter and hardly any income, become willing converts to his faith. And then these converts get trained as warriors. We know now that most of his followers are no bhaktas but trained warriors in the guise of bhaktas.'

'But why would Basava do that?' asked the King, eyebrows raised in either genuine or mock surprise.

'We believe there is a plot to overthrow your rule and make Basava the king,' said Mancharasa and paused suddenly, unsure if he should continue. When the king pouted and shook his head as if to say he did not know what to say, he continued, 'People are confused, Your Majesty. They do not know what is right and what is wrong. Basavanna could prove to be dangerous. You should do something fast.'

Bijjala nodded but did not speak. He now looked at Pandit Sharma, who had been specially summoned to the meeting.

Pandit Sharma was not part of Mancharasa's team. He was a man of vast learning and an authority on the Vedas, who did not see eye to eye with the Shastris and Dikshits of Kalyana. In fact, he stayed clear of the different sects of Brahmins and led the lonely life of a maverick scholar. Wracked by diseases of old age, he looked shrivelled up like an ancient tree. But his mind was still razor sharp. He sat crouched in his seat, glaring at Shastri whom he hated most. Presently, at the signal of the king, he spoke from his seat.

'I do not understand what these people are saying; rather, I should say I do not accept their interpretation of the Vedas and our sacred tradition. *I am a Brahmin*, but I don't belong to any caste. The word *Brahmin* does not refer to a caste, it is not a common noun under which you can include all kinds of beasts. Yes, a Brahmin is one who seeks *Brahman*, one who has chosen to live the life of poverty but engaged in constant search of truth. Yes, he is also the interpreter of the sacred Vedas, but not (pointing at Shastri) like them, and not like the priests who roam this land like wolves in the forest, preying on weak minds.'

He paused, breathing hoarsely, and then pushing himself up a little against the backrest, he continued.

'I don't know what the problem with Basava is. I haven't met him and I don't care to. But I believe he is a Brahmin by birth and he has betrayed his calling as a Brahmin. I don't accept his criticism of Brahmins. A true Brahmin is beyond castes, sects and the many social practices that go in the name of faith. These temples and monasteries are not the creations of Brahmins. What has a Brahmin got to do with temples? Absolutely nothing. Temple priests, funeral and wedding priests, cannot be called Brahmins. All these are mere professions to make a living, not the true vocation a Brahmin is meant to pursue. True Brahmins like me do our prayers and perform our rituals and pursue knowledge at home, never in temples. Temples are creations of kshatriyas and priests and Kings.'

He paused again, feeling almost exhausted by speaking. Devarasa quickly brought him drinking water in a silver tumbler. Pandit Sharma drank from it, making a deep gurgling sound.

'So you don't accept them as Brahmins?' asked the king, pointing at Shastri and Damodara who were looking away, avoiding Sharma's eyes.

'Listen,' said the old man, his voice getting even more hoarse, 'A true Brahmin is one who lives by the spirit of the Vedas. The Vedas lay down the rules and order by which a true Brahmin lives, by performing rituals and making his offerings. And remember, these rituals and the mantras have mystic meaning and significance connected to the cosmic forces and events that petty minds cannot grasp.'

He paused again, tired and ill at ease as if he had expressed the inexpressible. 'Now enough of all this debate.

I have said what I wanted to. There are not many Brahmins left in the world today. Their number is dwindling by the day, which only means the Kali Yuga is round the corner.'

Breathing hard and turning red in the face, Shastri burst out, 'You have no right to criticize or pass judgement about others, when your own son has turned his back on you and joined Basava.'

'What do you say to that?' asked Damodar, grinning wickedly.

'Is that true?' asked the King, looking surprised.

'He is no more my son,' cried the Pandit, his voice little more than a croak. 'The fool never understood his sacred calling and has now lost his Brahminhood. He has failed as a Brahmin and failed as my son. I have given instructions that after I die, he shall not perform the funeral rites.'

The next day, Bijjala sent word for Basava.

'What is this Basavanna,' he said, looking distressed. 'I hear so many complaints against you and your people. I hope they are not true.'

And then, upon Bijjala's signal, his most trusted minister and confidante, Devarasa, listed the allegations against Basava.

'I expected something like this to happen much earlier,' Basava said, unsurprised but smiling sadly. 'Now my only request to you is that you must kindly call all these people and we will thrash out these issues openly.'

He paused, expecting some reaction and as there was none, he continued, with an edge to his voice. 'Perhaps, they all see me as their enemy, but I do not see them as such. I'm not against Brahmins, why should I be? True, I'm critical of their caste practices and their self-assumed authority over religious matters...'

'You are getting angry,' remarked the king.

'I think you should visit our place and see for yourself what is happening there. I'm not interested in power of any kind. My way is not the way of politics, not the way of power.'

'But, Basavanna,' Devarasa intervened, as if waiting for a chance to pounce upon Basava, 'by telling the shudras and even the ati-shudras that they are equal to Brahmins and Kshatriyas and other castes, you have given them power over others. Isn't that politics?'

'Not power over others,' replied Basava, tersely, 'but power over themselves. It is a matter of rediscovering their equality and dignity in life, which had been denied to them all these ages. It is an insult to God to call or treat someone as "low" and some as "high". We are all equal before God.'

'But what you are saying goes against the sacred shastras and scriptures!' insisted Devarasa.

'And then, Basavanna,' he continued, in a rather strident voice, 'don't you see that your talk of equality and your support to the shudras have only made them arrogant and scornful towards others. Take the case of your washerman, Machayya. I'm told that he not only refuses to wash the clothes of people other than saranas, I believe he now goes around the streets of the Brahmin locality shouting that he'd never wash their dirty clothes, not even those of the royal family.'

Basava could not help smiling. He did not want to discuss Machayya's understandable, rather, praiseworthy rebellion. He simply said, 'I should tell you that I have read the religious texts as closely and seriously as anybody else. I can quote from them to prove that they do not sanction the chaturvarna system. But then, to me, shastras or scriptures are not the ultimate authority. We should go by our experience, by what we see and experience in actuality, and not by what is written in some text, however sacred.'

'Experience! Yes, I agree there,' gushed Bijjala. 'All our spiritual masters have said the same thing.'

Devarasa looked at the king, unsure as to whether he should continue or stop; but when he saw Bijjala wink and smile at him, he resumed his interrogation.

'Excuse me, Basavanna,' he said, drawing Basava's attention again. 'In one of your vachanas you have said that the one who does not wear the linga on his body is a *holeya*, an untouchable. Is that correct?'

Basava looked confused for a moment, and then with a gentle laugh, he answered, 'The vachanas are composed in particular contexts and they have to be understood in those contexts. But then, I have also said that the one who tells lies, steals and kills is a holeya. Only those who speak truth and who wish and work for the good of humanity are of noble castes.'

'But still the one without the linga is an untouchable, right?' Devarasa persisted.

'Yes, but that is so in a manner of speaking; it is to emphasize the spiritual importance of wearing the linga. I mean it is a way of saying that bereft of the linga and bhakti, the one who is wallowing in power, wealth and ignorance, is in fact an untouchable.'

Bijjala blinked and narrowed his eyes to slits.

'Power?' Devarasa frowned and his mouth curled into a snarl. 'You don't mean to include our Maharaja?'

'No, I don't mean to include our Maharaja,' Basava answered coolly. 'But I mean to include all those who tread the path of worldly pleasure and power, all those who shut their eyes and minds to the mystery and miracle of Shiva, and all those who in their arrogance think that they are highborn and learned but in reality know nothing.'

Bijjala chuckled, as if what Basava said was a joke. Then he spoke gravely, 'Basavanna, that is a pretty long definition of holeya. And it seems to include all of us, poor mortals.'

'Your Majesty,' Basava started respectfully, yet in a voice charged with emotion, 'isn't the mind witness enough for the taste on the tongue? Is it necessary to bring out the texts to support everything?'

Bijjala laughed, and then launched into a long advisory speech. And he was tactful.

'Basavanna, sometimes I don't understand what you are saying. But I know you are a good man and you have the good of the people in your heart. That is surely an admirable quality. But you cannot knock down hundreds-of-years-old traditions that have the sanction of the sacred texts and our elders. Do your good work, Basava, but do not make enemies. I know you don't see anyone as your enemy. That is your goodness. But you already have more enemies than you could count on your fingertips and that is not good. I like you and you are my most capable and efficient minister. Just see that you do not push things too far. You know, even nectar when consumed too much could turn poisonous.'

The King was magnificent, even Basava had to admit it. But now it was his turn to laugh and he laughed gently and replied tersely: 'I only know that I am a Shiva-bhakta and that I say and do what the Lord bids me to say and do.'

Since there was nothing more to say, Basava stood up from his chair to leave.

'Basavanna,' Devarasa said sharply, 'one last question. I have observed that you do not actually bow to the Maharaja, but bow to the image of the Shiva-linga on your finger-ring. What does that mean? Disregard for the Maharaja? Or, do you question the authority of the Maharaja?'

Basava took some time to answer. He shut his eyes for a while as if in deep meditation, and then opening his eyes and smiling, he told him, 'I bow only to Lord Shiva. I don't mean disrespect to our Maharaja. I work under him; he is my master and my King, but not my God. Kings come and go and they serve a need. We have created a world where kings and governments are considered necessary. Otherwise there could be anarchy and danger. But a time will come, and when it comes, we shall be in no need of kings and states. We should work towards building such an enlightened society. I'm sure our Maharaja would agree that the king's role lies in creating such a world where Dharma and peace will reign supreme.'

No sooner had Basava left the chamber than Devarasa, looking distraught, muttered, 'Your Majesty, Basavanna could make trouble for you.'

Bijjala laughed, but deep in his heart he too was worried.

'He is a good man, Devarasa,' Bijjala said. 'He means no harm and there is no danger. And Devarasa, haven't you read your history? Many such crazy people have passed through all ages. We just have to leave them alone and no harm will come.'

'But, Your Majesty,' Devarasa persisted, 'we can never be sure how things will turn out in the long run. We cannot take the risk...'

With a wave of his hand, Bijjala stopped him and asked, 'Haven't you heard of one Allama Prabhu? He is the craziest of the lot. He not only trashes and rejects all forms of authority, including kings, I believe he makes mincemeat of even gods and goddesses. What do you say to that? Put him and such crazy people in prison and create unrest in society?'

That evening Neela visited the king, clad in a simple cotton sari, and Bijjala noticed that she wore no jewels. For a moment, it seemed to Bijjala that she had come deliberately dressed that way to insult him. She did not smile, nor greet him, and that annoyed him further. Yet, controlling his anger, he said, 'I thought you have forgotten you have a brother.'

'I may forget a brother,' Neela reacted coldly, 'but how can I forget the King? Or, should I say the most glorious, unconquerable, unparalleled emperor!'

'There's no need for sarcasm, my dear girl,' said Bijjala, getting angry.

And Neela spoke bluntly.

'I'm upset about the false accusations levelled against my husband and the way he was interrogated, as if he were a common criminal. It is like finding fault with the sun for lighting up the world and showering his grace over thieves and saints alike. He is not just my husband but my guru as well. I have learnt many things at his feet. And I know that all he wants to do is to free us from our ignorant and superstitious ways of living and find our liberation through our Lord.'

'I can see that you have become an ardent follower of your husband,' Bijjala said, amused by her audacity. 'But, are you happy?'

'Brother, I'm more than happy. And I thank you for marrying me to one so noble and wise. I feel truly blessed. But, brother, we need your love and support. You are yourself a worshipper of Lord Shiva. You should understand.'

'What do you want me to do?' asked Bijjala, laughing. 'Become a follower of your husband? Wear a linga on me and smear ash on my forehead?'

'What is wrong with that?' Neela asked in genuine wonder.

'I am the emperor; yes, the most glorious Emperor, as you rightly say,' Bijjala yelled, losing his calm. 'And I should look to the interests and welfare of all my people. I cannot look to favour one group or one person over another, however great and noble.'

Neela saw the king was upset. Dropping her voice and looking him in the eyes, she pleaded, 'Brother, it is just that I pray you do not go by what people say about Basavanna. I know there are many who don't like him.'

'Did Basavanna send you?'

'No,' said Neela, face flushed with embarrassment. 'He does not know that I am here. But I'll tell him when I return. There are no secrets between us.'

His face knotted with doubts and questions he would not discuss, Bijjala paced the room back and forth. He sighed, he smiled, and he said, 'I understand, but let us not discuss this matter further. There are far more important issues for me to worry about.' And then he went over to where she stood and laying his hand affectionately on her shoulder, said, 'Come, let's go in and meet others. Don't forget you are one of us.' And as they moved towards an inner chamber, he asked, though with some hesitation, 'But why are you dressed like this, like a village woman?'

A little distance away from the sangama, where the two rivers joined, facing the ancient temple of Lord Sangameshvara, on a raised platform stood Bahurupi. A young and shy sun hovered somewhere in the background and a cold breeze came from the river. It was the month of karthika, and almost every evening it rained and the nights became chilly. So, Bahurupi and Nage gave their performances in the mornings.

Since Basava left Kappadisangama, nearly sixteen years ago, a sea change had come over the region. A large number of families there had become followers of Basava. Even the many Brahmins of the region had taken to the new faith. Ishanya Guru, Basava's first and only guru, was no more. In his place, Shivaguna, once a fellow student of Basava, had become the head of the matha.

That morning, dressed like Basava in a turban, a loose top and a dhoti, and his forehead smeared with holy ash, Bahurupi narrated the story of Basava's many encounters with the shudra communities. He gave a vivid account of Basava's meeting with Haralayya, the leader of the tanner community, and how Haralayya and his wife, Suguna, after much debate and long deliberations with Basava, took to the path of Shiva. Then he told them about the theft in Mahamane, something that amused the crowd no end. One night, a thief, who was of course never caught, —who knows, it could have been one of the saranas working in the house— made good with most of the jewels that belonged to both Neela and Ganga. The next day morning, on learning about the theft of the jewels, Basava reprimanded his wives, saying, 'What a shame! I would have been much happier if you had yourselves given away the jewels!'

'Call the thief,' said Ganga, not entirely jokingly, 'I believe the thief forgot to look into the puja room.'

Just as the crowd broke into little guffaws, some even praising the selfless and noble character of Basava and admiring Ganga's delightful irony, Bahurupi stunned them with the news of the death of Basava's son.

'Basava was in the tanner's colony when the news of his son's death was brought to him. Sitting outside Haralayya's house, which had been swept clean of animal skin, Basava was explaining kayaka, the notion of work, as an act of devotion and offering to the Lord, when Kinari Bommanna came and stood at a distance, looking pale and arms folded over his almost bony chest. Basava threw a cursory glance at Bommanna, but did not stop speaking. Some time passed and when still there was no sign of Basava finishing his talk, Bommanna burst out, "Basava, your son is no more."

'"Shivaa…" cried Basava and shut his eyes. Haralayya and others did not know how to react, what to say, stunned as they were by the terrible news. Basava's face remained placid as in meditation for several moments and then the tears spilled over and trickled down his cheeks. He opened his eyes, wiped the tears with his shawl and stood up. Nobody uttered a word. Even Suguna, Haralayya's wife, a warm-hearted yet outspoken woman, said nothing, but her eyes too were filled with tears. What could they say? Suddenly, words had lost their meaning, words that had been used to such great effect only a few moments earlier. In silent communion, the little group of tanners followed Basava to his house.

'A large crowd of saranas had already gathered outside the Great Mansion. Braving a scorching sun, they stood in clusters, speaking in whispers. Inside, senior saranas sat huddled in corners, in gloomy silence. The ten-year-old bubbly little fellow had been a source of such joy! For a young boy he had phenomenal memory. He could recite accurately vachanas he had heard just once. He was a stout little fellow with chubby cheeks, and a cleft chin, like his father, and had large brown eyes of his mother, Ganga, who now sat by his body, downcast, without shedding a tear, but her face contorted with agony she would not give vent to. But, Neela, who was sitting by her side, convulsed with sobs.

'When Basava strode in, his face wracked in pain, it was Neela who rose and fell on his shoulder, crying uncontrollably. Ganga did not move, did not as much as lift her head to see her husband.

'The sight of his son's dead body, and Ganga sitting by the corpse and suffering in silence, tore at his heart.

'"Shiva," he gasped and, choking on his words, muttered, "Mysterious is the way of our Lord."'

Narrating the tragic event, his own eyes now a pool of tears, Bahurupi asked:

'Dear brothers and sisters, tell me, is it possible not to be affected by death, death of your near and dear ones, especially your own child? How did Basava and his two wives cope with the sudden death of their son? It is said that losing one's child is the greatest sorrow in life. But saranas say that Basava was least affected by the tragedy. I do not think it is entirely true. However, on the eleventh day of the boy's death, Neela and Ganga gave away gifts of food grains, clothes and cows, and all the gold and silver the thief had not been able to lay his hands on.

'"Shiva," Ganga prayed, "curse me to be born a barren woman in my next birth, if there is going to be one."

'"Take everything, my Lord," Basava said, "You give and You take. I am only a trustee."

And he plunged back into work.

'I believe the very next day he went to the tanner's colony to finish the unfinished conversation with Haralayya and his friends. You'll be surprised to know that Basava has not composed a single vachana on either his relationship with or loss of his son he affectionately called Putt Sangaiah. But Ganga was devastated. For months she hardly stirred out of the house and, except with Neela, she would not talk to anyone else, not even Basava.

'Strange are the ways of life, stranger still human relationships, especially the one between husband and wife. Four months after the death of Basava's son, one day, I went to meet and talk to Ganga. I was quite surprised to see that, unlike Neela and the women saranas who wore ochre-coloured saris, she was clad in white. And she wore no necklace of beads and her forehead was blank with no holy ash, not even kumkum. She did not of course look to be in sorrow, but she was no more the high-spirited, cheerful self that she had been before the death of her son. She had changed. But, clad in white, that day, she looked the picture of a strange yogini.

'I said, "Mother, can I speak a few words with you?"

'"There is no need to be so formal, Bahurupi. I know you and I know why you want to talk to me," she said, putting me at ease.

'So, without beating around the bush, I asked her how she had been able to cope with the irreparable loss of her son, but she did not let me finish, and what she said I'll never forget.

'"There are only two things a mother can do," she said, "one, love her child as if there is no tomorrow, and once the child is gone, learn to live as if there was no yesterday." She smiled a smile of supreme understanding, but it was not without the touch of sorrow.'

Allama meets Muktayi and Siddarama

The moon was in the clouds and a soft breeze played about like a friendly spirit. A huge owl flew over the whispering trees and perched on the highest branch. It looked down at the blazing light, with its large-brown unblinking eyes, as if in wonder at the ways of human beings. Bahurupi was dressed differently that night. He looked like a beggar in tatters, but he was smiling, showing his fine white teeth. But, of course, the crowd instantly knew whom Bahurupi was imitating, though they had no clue to what was coming.

Caressing his fake beard and grinning impishly, Bahurupi said:

'I don't know. Believe me, I'm more confused than you people. I'm not a man of knowledge, much less a wise man. I have many questions the answers to which I have not found, and the answers I have found have, strange as it may sound, led me to still more knotty questions and confusion. That is what happens when you meet Allama, and when you have as your friend a person like Nage.

'You cannot trust your eyes or your ears. You cannot trust your own mind. This really is a ridiculous situation you find yourself in. But then, you know that it is through your mind you see and experience the world. It is through thought that you think who and what you are. It is through thought you see, analyse, experience, and interpret your life and the life around you. And it is again through thought you look at your other thoughts and wonder where all this is coming from and where all this is going to end.

'But Allama insists: trust not your mind. He says the mind is the mischief-maker and the mischief. The mind is what you are. The mind is like a river that is never still, and it is all maya. Unless the mind becomes empty, declares our Allama, you really cannot see or know and understand anything.

'Friends, I cannot claim to have understood what Allama says. It is all really intriguing. How does one empty the mind? And, pray, who is going to empty the mind? Can the mind empty itself? I have no clue and yet, I must ask: why empty the mind? To empty the mind is to flush out all our stories from time immemorial, isn't it? And what will I do with an empty mind? Think about it. But don't tell Allama that I said this,' he laughed and continued, 'Oh, I love stories, otherwise I wouldn't be here and you wouldn't be sitting there, listening. Anyway, having said that, now, I must get on with Allama's story.

'You know, the whereabouts of Allama is always a mystery. Today he is here, tomorrow he is gone and you have no idea where. But this time, we know—at least I hope this is true—that, along with Siddarama, he is on his way to Kalyana. Last week, Nage and I were in Siddarama's village, Sonnallige, and that is where we learnt all about Allama's meeting with Siddarama and their journey together to Kalyana. But before meeting Siddarama, he met Muktayakka. And you must know that Muktayakka is the sister of our great Ajagana.

'Ajagana was a devotee of Shiva, and a strange mystic. Mystics are always strange, anyway. From the age of sixteen, bewildering changes started coming over Ajagana. We do not know much about that. And we do not know how he came to wear the linga, or if a guru initiated him. His father, who was a worshipper of Lord Vishnu, did not approve of this sudden and extreme change in him. But Ajagana did not care. Early one morning, he left home, took a dip in the lake and went and sat on the steps of the Shiva temple. He never went back home until after the death of his father. He would not go into the temple for darshana or to offer puja, but just squat on the steps, staring at the world with vacant eyes. Whatever offerings the temple devotees gave him would be his meal for the day.

'One day, upset and angry, the father came to the temple and shouted at his son to go back home with him. Ajagana only blinked and not a muscle moved in his body. The father lost his mind and started beating his son in front of everyone. Still, the boy showed no sign of emotion, let alone get up and follow his father back home. That night, the father died and nobody could make out the cause of his death. Soon the news spread in the village that the boy possessed supernatural powers.

'Ajagana rarely spoke, but when he spoke it was always on mundane things, never on spiritual matters; probably because to him it was something deeply personal and sacred and not something to be talked about. My guess is of course as good as yours. However, as days passed, many began to think that he was just plain mad, but there were a few in the village who believed he was a spiritually advanced person. Those few were the ones who helped Muktayi, Ajagana's sister, to support herself and her brother. Their mother had died a few years before the father's sudden demise. After their father's death, Muktayi became Ajagana's mother, sister, friend and disciple—all rolled into one. In the morning, she would go to the temple, offer her puja to the God and prasada to her brother, come home to milk the cow and then cook a simple meal for herself. Some nights Ajagana would eat a frugal meal at home, and occasionally, share his strange experiences and visions with Muktayi.

'Years rolled by, but nothing much changed in Ajagana's routine. However, Muktayi grew into a mature woman, intellectually and spiritually, and she even started composing vachanas, which sometimes she would recite to her brother. She was now looked upon as a deeply spiritual person and was addressed as Muktayakka, even by the elders of the village. Jangamas, who passed through the village, would sometimes, accepting her hospitality, share food with the brother and sister and spend the night in their house.

'We do not know what went on inside of Ajagana's mind and body, what changes took place. He hardly composed vachanas and never spoke about himself. He was a strange yogi, whose life was like that of a ship traversing through uncharted sea, with no record of its journey left behind. Whatever little we know is from the reports of his sister. Indeed, she was a witness to the weird changes happening to her brother. One day he would forget her name, and even who he was. Another day he would call her and complain that his body was missing. At times, he would sit up and start speaking into blank space, or with some apparition only he could see, or chant hymns in praise of Lord Shiva. It was all too weird and terribly confusing and confounding to Muktayakka. But she carried on her watch, and taking care of Ajagana as if he were her overgrown child.

'One day, however, things went beyond her understanding and control. It so happened that Ajagana could not swallow food. At first he thought the rice was too hot, since it burned his fingers and throat. Muktayakka was shocked. The rice had been cooked an hour earlier and it was anything but hot. The heat came not from outside, but was boiling up inside Ajagana's body. The burning increased and spread all over his body. It was as if he had swallowed fire and it was raging inside of him, burning every muscle, every bone and nerve. The whole day he kept rolling on the floor, unable to withstand the intense heat.

'Ajagana did not want her sister to call for a vaidya. It was no ordinary fever or illness, but something very strange was happening to his body. It was Shiva's doing, he said, and was willing to suffer the process. Muktayakka too believed that what was happening to her brother was something profoundly spiritual, but of which she had no clue. Night came and Ajagana could not stand the torture anymore. He thought he was going to die.

'" It is all too much," he told his sister. "These monstrous waves of energy can't be contained by this little frame of flesh and bones. I do not know why the Lord is burning me up. This is the end. I think my time has come. Do not grieve over my passing away. Where would I go but to the abode of our Lord."

'Then he sat up and asked for some water to drink. Muktayakka gave him a tumbler of water and stood aside, chanting the name of the Lord. Ajagana drank the water in quick small draughts and then, as Muktayakka kept chanting and watching in bewilderment, he removed his ishtalinga, which had been wrapped in a piece of cloth, and chanting *Om namah-shivaya*, swallowed it.

'Muktayakka sat by the grave of Ajagana, her eyes swollen from crying, her hair dishevelled, face wracked in unbearable grief. After three days she briefly raised her eyes and saw an apparition of a man in rags, an unkempt beard and long hair. She thought he was some wanderer who had drifted into the graveyard, and she withdrew into her suffering self. The man did not leave; he moved closer to the grave. Now, puzzled, Muktayakka looked up again and saw him smiling. She saw the smile break into a hoarse laughter.

'As if slapped in the face, Muktayakka whipped her head up and asked, "What are you laughing at?"

'"I was wondering," said the man, "what is it that you are crying and suffering so much about? Is it because your brother ended his life suddenly and left you alone? Tell me, are you weeping for your brother, or for yourself?"

'The strange authority with which the man spoke upset Muktayakka.

'"Why should you know?" She snapped back at him. "What is your problem? Leave me alone and go your way."

'"This is my way," said the man, grinning mischievously.

'There was something really strange and intriguing about the man. He was surely no ordinary fellow, thought Muktayakka. She stood up, and adjusting her clothes and wiping the tears off her eyes, she asked, "Who are you?"

'"They call me Allama."

'Muktayakka had heard about Allama from the jangamas who had occasionally stayed in her house. But she could not associate what they had said of him with the man in rags standing in front of her. They had said that Allama was an unconventional Shiva-bhakta and a wandering guru, but a guru who had no wish to have any disciples.

'"Ajagana was not merely my brother," Muktayakka said, "he was my guru as well."

'"Aha!" said Allama. "So, losing a guru is a profound sorrow, but losing a brother is inconsequential, eh?"

'"I don't think you understand," Muktayakka reacted sharply, doubting if he was really the Allama she had heard about or some crazy pretender.

'"But why do you need a guru," Allama continued, rather rudely. "A guru misleads people, even when he or she happens to be your own brother or sister." He laughed, it seemed mockingly. "But let us not blame the gurus. The problem is with us, isn't it? We want others to lead us, guide us! Why? Why don't you just follow your own path, go by what your inner voice tells you?"

'"This must really be Allama!" Muktayakka thought to herself. "But why does he speak thus? Why is he so crude and cruel? How can he be a guru? He has no compassion."

'As if reading her thought, Allama spoke, "The so-called compassion of gurus is only a trick of egoism. They steal your hearts through their show of compassion and make you their slaves for life. Don't you understand? What a fool you are!"

'It was like another slap on her face and she reacted bitterly. "I think what I have heard about you is all false. You are a very arrogant man. You call compassion egoism? How can you? And for a guru you speak too much and too rudely. Perhaps you think no end of yourself!"

'"Of course I think no end of myself, for I have no beginning and therefore no end. And indeed I'm the most arrogant man on earth," replied Allama, shaking with laughter. And then caressing his long, shaggy beard, he said gravely, "If you must know, you cannot compare me with anyone. You have no idea. I'm above and beyond all your gurus either of the present or of the past. In my view, they are all fools, misguided fools. Even your gods are not equal to me, do you understand? All your gurus and gods are mere dust under my feet."

'Muktayakka could not believe her ears. This was no arrogance or egotism but something far too outrageous and vile, or, something beyond her comprehension. Who is this man really? Whoever or whatever he really is, decided Muktayakka, she was not going to be intimidated by him.

'"Don't think I'm impressed by your big and wild talk," she said. "I'm not. In fact, I find no reason why I should believe you or your words, or even listen to you."

'"Indeed, why should you!" said Allama. "But then, why should you believe your brother, or, for that matter, yourself either? Why don't you question your brother who is lodged in your mind as some terrible pain? And question yourself, too. Why do you suffer thus? Is this the way you want to live?"

'Muktayakka stared at Allama. She noticed that his eyes expressed no feelings, although he spoke so passionately, but were rather vacant; they just looked unblinkingly back at her.

She asked, "Why did you come here? Who are you really?"

'Allama laughed. "Is this how you treat your guest?" He tapped his sunken stomach, and said, "I have not eaten a meal for the last two days."

'Muktayakka broke into a smile, embarrassed, yet, feeling strangely light-hearted. "Come," she said, forgetting all her sorrow, as one with some new-found excitement. "We'll go home and I'll cook a meal for you." '

That evening, Bahurupi was laid up with fever. Nage sat by him, placing a cold-water compress on him and trying to humour him.

'Maybe some profound spiritual change is taking place in you,' Nage teased, 'like it happened to Ajagana!'

'Forget it,' cried Bahurupi, 'I'm not going to kill myself, nor am I going to die of this silly fever. Now please let me rest quietly for some time.'

Bahurupi had wrapped himself in two blankets; yet he felt cold shivers now and then. Moments passed in silence. Studying Bahurupi's face and smiling, suddenly, as if it was too painful not to speak, Nage asked, 'What are you thinking so deeply about? Say something.'

'What else,' sighed Bahurupi, staring up at the wooden beams in the ceiling. 'Either I'm thinking of Allama, or I'm thinking of my wife. They both have made my life miserable.' And he drew the blankets over his head.

'Who is in your mind now?' asked Nage.

'Who else but my wife,' yelled Bahurupi from under the blankets. Then, putting his head out, he said, 'But you rascal, you never talk about yourself. For a change, why don't you say something about yourself?'

Nage never spoke about his life. Did he have a wife and children? Where was he born? Who were his parents? He would either laugh as a reply, or, grinning from ear to ear, burble thus: 'You know something, I was born out of Shiva's laughter. You'll not believe it, I know. But this is how it happened: One day, in Kailasa, Parvati said to Shiva, "Why is there so much sorrow in the world? It is really affecting me, my Lord. I feel so hopelessly depressed. You must do something." In response, Shiva started to giggle and soon the giggle grew into a roaring, apocalyptic laughter and out of that terrific laughter I was born here on earth.'

The next morning, Nage took Bahurupi's place to tell the story of Siddarama. He was dressed up not as Allama, nor as Siddarama, but as Bahurupi, with a loose top, half-dhoti, and a green turban.

He began in a voice that sounded surprisingly like that of Bahurupi. And his style of narration, too, was not very different from that of his friend. In fact, Nage's imitation of Bahurupi was so nearly perfect that Bahurupi, who sat amongst the crowd, wrapped in a thick sheet like a peasant, wondered where Nage was and why he had left him alone on the stage.

Adopting the guise and manner of Bahurupi, Nage said, 'Ignorance is really bliss; you know why, because the more you know the more you find yourself in confusion. Siddarama knew that too well, and he knew all the tricks of the mind.

'Brothers and sisters, you must know that Siddarama was no ordinary sadhaka. He had travelled widely and met people from all walks of life. He had visited Srishaila and spent three years worshipping Lord Chennamalikarjuna with single-minded devotion. Later, he had done vigorous tapas in the forest of Banavasi for several years. But with all these relentless sadhana, he was honest enough to admit to himself, and to those who cared to listen to him, that the core of him had not been touched by his long and rigorous study and tapas. He was the same old person given to conflict, jealousy, frustration, anger and lust. There seemed to be no escape from passions he so desperately struggled to free himself from. Several months passed in sheer agony and then one day, he hit upon the solution to the problem. The only trick to neutralise the cunning mind was to never let it raise its chatty, ugly head and play mischief. Kayaka, work with undivided devotion, was that trick. Work, work, and work so that the mind will stay focussed on the task at hand; work until you fall asleep.

'Friends, the problem with the mind does not lie in thinking as such, does not lie in talking as such. The problem lies in thinking to oneself, in talking to oneself. This constant chatter of the mind with itself is the mischief, the problem that unsettles the rhythm of life, that fragments, divides life into this and that, into I and you, us and them and so on. So, Siddarama, in order to silence this ever-chattering mind, plunged himself into relentless work. Work became his mantra and the worship of Lord Shiva. And he did great work that enormously benefited the people of Sonnallige. The villagers adored and worshipped him as their benefactor, liberator and Guru. With the help of his followers and villagers, he got houses built for those who had no proper shelter, wells dug and huge tanks built that solved the problem of water in the drought-prone region. He promoted cooperative farming and in five years time there was hardly any poor family living in Sonnallige. Thus, our Siddarama initiated a revolution of sorts in the region that transformed the lives of thousands of families.

'At the time of Allama's arrival in Sonnallige, Siddarama was engaged in the construction of two new buildings, next to the matha. One was to be used as a shelter for travellers and the other for starting a school. Bare-bodied, dhoti wrapped around his thighs, he worked along with labourers.

'Approaching the construction site, Allama went near a group of workers and yelled, "Who among you is the leader?"

'A thin-looking, middle-aged man came forward. "Swami, what can I do for you?"

'"You are not Siddarama, are you?" said Allama, frowning. "Call that idler here. I want to speak to him."

'Shocked, the man gaped at Allama's beggarly guise. To him Allama looked a fake sanyasi, a false jangama trying to take advantage of the now legendary hospitality of Siddarama. He could not be too sure, though; but then, even if the stranger were a thief, Siddarama would not have approved of him treating the stranger harshly. So, controlling his anger, he said, "Swami, if there is one person who is wholly selfless and hardworking in Sonnallige and in the eight villages and two towns around this place, it is our Guru Siddarama."

'By then, on hearing about the stranger, Siddarama himself came running to the spot. Looking at Allama, he knew instantly that the stranger was no ordinary jangama.

'"Swami," he said, "I'm Siddarama."

'Allama considered Siddarama for a while, he stared at his bare chest glistening with sweat, at his soiled hands and mud-caked feet, and then said harshly, "You think you are a simple and humble man because you work with your labourers and pretend to look like one of them? What kind of a guru are you?"

'A few more workers had by now stopped their work and gathered around the stranger. They could not believe that somebody could speak so rudely and insultingly to their Guru. Siddarama himself was stunned by the sudden attack. But he had seen and met enough people in life not to be upset by the stranger's rude remark.

'He smiled and said, "Swami, I am a labourer. God's own labourer, nothing more, nothing less."

'If many in the crowd were quite outraged by the stranger's remark, a few among them were now irritated with their Guru's polite answer as well. For they thought Guru Siddarama should not be so very humble and vulnerable that any fool could take advantage of his goodness.

'As the stranger did not respond and kept staring at him with unblinking eyes, Siddarama asked softly, politely, "Swami, may I know who you are and where you are from?"

'"Does it really matter?" Allama roared in reply. 'If I'm a woman killer, is your response going to change? If I'm Lord Shiva himself in the flesh, are you going to be more respectful?"

'Siddarama brought his palms together in great show of humility. 'Swami, please forgive my impertinence. Tell me, what I can do for you. I'm at your service."

'"Tell me," asked Allama, in the same rude tone, "how much have you dug and how much have you constructed? And tell me honestly, have you found what you have been searching for?"

'His palms still joined in respect, Siddarama answered, "Swami, what can I say? I have dug enough to know that I'm not the doer, and I have constructed enough to realize that there is nothing permanent. And Swami, I can't say I have found what I wanted, or that my search has ended. I don't know. I don't want to know."

'"You are tired and afraid, Siddarama," said Allama, no longer angry or harsh but with kindly affection. "But, still, you have not given up your pride. You have not given up your hope. The mind is a very tricky customer, Siddarama." And then, raising his finger and raising his voice, Allama said, 'Feed the poor, tell the truth, make water places for the thirsty and build tanks for a town. You may go to heaven after death, but you'll be nowhere near the truth of our Lord. And the man who knows our Lord, he gets no results.'

'The people around were quite intrigued by this sudden change of tone in the conversation between their master and the stranger, more so at the stranger who seemed to exercise a great influence on their master. As they stood wondering, watching and listening to the stranger's admonition that sounded like a vachana, they saw their guru go down on his knees and then looking up with reverence at the stranger, speak in a trembling voice: "I know who you are! Forgive me for not recognising you before. Forgive and bless us, Allama Prabhu."

'"O Allama Prabhu...Prabhu Allama," chanted the crowd after Siddarama, though many of them did not know who Allama was.'

A Nameless Thief and Gowravva

Bathed in the soft moonlight, trees stood still as in deep thought, and on their many branches slept many birds of many hues. In a clearing, a lone wolf, its fluffy tail aslant, raised its head and sniffed at the moon. It was the night of the full moon. Inside the old, ruined temple, in one corner of what was at one time the sanctum sanctorum, slept Mahadevi. There was no idol of God. The pedestal, bare and broken, looked like a man squatting in the middle of the room. By the side of it stood two real men, studying Mahadevi in the dim light that trickled down through the wide cracks in the roof.

Like an animal sensing danger, Mahadevi opened her eyes and saw the two figures, like fleshed up shadows, hovering over her. She sat up but did not move. This had to happen one day or the other, she knew. And she knew now there was no way she could fight these men off if they were to pounce upon her.

'So this is it,' she thought and braced herself to face the situation. She was not afraid, but she felt a strange discomfort in her belly, something like a cramp. She looked up at the two menacing shadows and said, 'Brothers, what do you want?'

Grinning, one of the men said, 'What does a man want of a woman at this hour of the night?'

'Come on, let's have some fun. It's a beautiful night!' said the other man, who now, moving closer, squatted by her side and placed a hand on her naked shoulder.

Mahadevi did not move, did not flinch, but gently pushed his hand away. Then she turned and faced him.

'Brother, why do you speak thus to this woman with withered face and shrunken body? This body is of no use to you.'

The man by her side gaped at her nakedness in the dark. What was she saying? The other man who was still standing laughed. He took a step forward.

'Why do you speak like an old woman who is finished with life? You are so young and beautiful! Any man would happily give his right hand to have you!'

'Brother,' Mahadevi reacted quietly, 'I have lost all ties with this world. I have lain with Lord Chennamalikarjuna and lost my womanhood. Why bother with this woman who is no woman?'

The two men stared at each other in bewilderment. They could not see her face clearly in the dim light, but they detected no fear in her voice and that was quite unsettling. The man moved closer and bending down he peered closely at Mahadevi and then he knelt down in front of her.

'Aye, woman, stop talking as if you are some bodiless spirit. Come on now, lie down quietly and we'll not harm you.'

'Leave her alone,' a voice boomed across the room and the two men froze in fear. A tall and huge figure of a man stood at the doorless entrance, a long staff held in his right hand. As the bulky figure moved threateningly close, the two men leapt to their feet and scurried out of the room, muttering abuses.

Mahadevi looked at the man, wondering if he was someone she knew. In the shaft of light that fell on him from the cracked roof, she could see that he really was a huge fellow, with a long beard and in a long ochre robe. Could he be a jangama?

'Brother, who are you?' She asked, 'I'm much beholden to you.'

'I'm a thief,' replied the man. 'And I take on different avatars to deceive people.'

'Brother,' Mahadevi said, amazed, 'I admire your honesty. But I'm sorry I have nothing to offer you.'

A wry smile appeared on his face.

'When I first saw you, I did want to steal something from you,' he confessed. 'For two days I followed you closely like an animal. But you really are something! I don't know how it happened. My desire for you was replaced by a great curiosity to know you. This morning, when I saw you eating the wild berries, I wanted to come and stop you. These wild berries can be quite harmful sometimes, you never know. Then I thought I'll get some fruits for you and so I fell behind.'

He wandered about and found a mango grove, he said. He plucked a few half-ripe and some ripe mangoes and rushed back, only to find Mahadevi gone. Walking here and there the whole day in search of her, feeling desperate and angry with himself for having lost her, he had arrived at the temple and decided to spend the night there. That is when he had heard voices coming from inside and had sneaked in and found Mahadevi in trouble.

He stepped forward and placed the bunch of mangoes on the floor before her. 'Please accept them,' he said.

Mahadevi peered at his thickly bearded face in the faint light and said quietly, 'Brother, you are one with a good heart. You are very kind and I'm truly grateful to you. But why did you pluck so many mangoes? My needs are frugal.'

Moved, the man brought his palms together in deep respect. He said, 'I have neither seen nor met anyone like you in my whole life. In the last two days, I have felt like the hunter who has become the hunted. Pray, tell me, who are you?'

❖ ❖ ❖

The next day morning, there was no trace of either the thief or the two men. The thief had left the mangoes behind. Mahadevi offered her prayer to Lord Chennamalikarjuna and then picked a ripe golden yellow mango and bit into it. It seemed to her that she had never tasted so delicious a fruit before. She smiled to herself for the first time in several months. And she thought of the good thief with gratitude.

Remembering the previous night's conversation with the thief, she marvelled at his intelligence and the honesty with which he had spoken. After listening to her story, he had said, 'My parents, my wife and almost all my family members believe in God and they worship Devi. But I have never believed in God, nor have I felt the need for any faith. And I don't believe in these religious characters either. I think they are all a bunch of exploiters taking advantage of the credulity of the people. But, after listening to you, I guess there is something more to God and faith than what these people in ochre robes say.'

'How come you are a thief?'

'Oh, there is no mystery in it. I come from a family of thieves. My father was a thief, my grandfather was a thief, you see. There is no shame in this profession. I have never felt guilty of robbing people.'

'You are a strange person!'

'No, I'm not. It is you who is very strange. There are hundreds and thousands of thieves like me. But tell me, in a way, isn't everyone a thief? Aren't all of us thieves? Don't we all hanker after things we don't have and take what originally didn't belong to us? How does a rich man become rich, a Pandit become a Pandit, even a King become a King? How else do you think Bijjala became the emperor?'

'What belongs to us then?'

'Nothing. Absolutely nothing. So we steal, steal from each other and from mother earth. Some steal more than what they need and then there are many who haven't learnt the art of stealing and so remain poor and helpless. So you see, we are all stealers, there is no other way of living. But I only steal, I don't kill. Killing is another matter.'

'So nothing belongs to us?'

'I know why you ask. I remember you saying that nothing belongs to you, but that you belong to your Lord Chennamalikarjuna. I can't say the same. Yes, nothing belongs to me, so I take what I want; but I belong to my parents, my wife and five sons and three daughters whom I love dearly.' At that point he had suddenly stood up as if he had spoken too much and said, 'You must sleep now. You have a long way to go. Have no fear; sleep well. I'll be outside and no harm will come to you.'

The twilight lay on the land like a silent prayer when Mahadevi resumed her journey. She walked through the open field, chanting the name of her Lord in her mind. As the first light of the sun swept over the land, Mahadevi felt engulfed by a strange sense of joy. Last night's episode now seemed like a strange dream dreamt in another life. A faint smile creased her lips and slowly a vachana began to take shape in her mind:

> *When I didn't know myself,*
> *where were you?*
> *Like the colour in the gold,*
> *weren't you in me?*
> *I saw in you,*
> *O Lord Chennamalikarjuna,*
> *the paradox of your being in me*
> *without showing a limb.*

Against the vast brown and green field, her nakedness covered by her thick, long hair, moving in a slow, steady pace, she looked an image of a strange animal stealing its way through the field towards its destination. It was almost noon, but the sun had gone incognito. Masses of dark clouds had been gathering from the morning and now the sky turned a dark grey, and somewhere from the east, a heavy cold wind began to sweep across the field. Mahadevi paused for a while, and looking up at the sky that was fast turning gloomy, she prayed:

> *Not seeing you,*
> *in the hill, in the forest,*
> *from tree to tree,*
> *I roamed,*
> *searching, crying: Lord, my Lord,*
> *where is your kindness?*
> *Give me a clue to your hiding place,*
> *come, show me your face,*
> *O Lord Chennamalikarjuna.*

All was still for a while; not a leaf, not a blade of grass moved; and then the sky rumbled and it broke open. The earth shook and the wind roared. Not far from the hills, peacocks unfurled their coloured tails and began a dance. Mahadevi moved on, unmindful of the shattering rain. Her hair stuck to her skin like a million muddy-brown leeches. Gathering the dripping wet hair in both hands, she tied a knot and tossed it behind. Like a dark serpent, it trembled and slithered on her back. Naked, breast-to-breast with the cosmos, she broke into a trot. Laughing, giggling, she ran like a little girl, like she had never run before, and with no destination, no goal in her mind, while the waters from the heavens poured merrily down in torrents.

An hour later, the rains relented, the wind withdrew, and the sky looked quiet like a child after a wild sport.

Mahadevi cheered at a flock of white herons cutting across the wet sky and she plodded on, avoiding puddles of water and heavy slush. Before long, at a distance, she saw a structure that looked like a temple and, by its side, two human figures. She trudged on, feeling sapped, breathless and thirsty. She did not remember how she reached the temple, or if she was carried there. When she opened her eyes, she saw a woman about as old as her mother, sitting by her side. She had a prominent black mole on her right cheek, and she was smiling kindly.

'What happened? Who are you?' The woman asked.

Outside the temple, the husband of the woman stood by his bullock cart, fidgeting, wondering about Mahadevi's strange appearance. The couple were on their way back home from their son's house in the neighbouring village, when the heavy rain had forced them to stop and take shelter in the temple. Just when the rain stopped and they were about to leave, they had seen Mahadevi stumbling across the muddy field and then suddenly falling down.

The old couple took Mahadevi home. Mahadevi was running a fever and was in no condition to continue her journey. But she refused to be treated by the village doctor.

'The fever will go,' she said. 'I'll not die, not so soon, not until I meet my Lord.'

The woman let Mahadevi rest in a room and she herself treated her with whatever she knew of the remedies for fever. The fever lasted for three days and three nights. The fourth morning, the fever gone, Mahadevi looked fully recovered, but not strong enough to resume her journey. In the last twenty days, after she had started out from Uduthadi, except for night halts, Mahadevi had walked continuously with hardly any rest. She needed to rest now and recoup herself. And for the second time in all these days, she broke her self-imposed silence and spoke of her life to the woman.

After a while into the conversation, the woman, Gowravva, for that was her name, asked hesitantly, 'If you won't misunderstand me, can I ask you a personal question.'

'There are no secrets in my life,' said Mahadevi, smiling.

'Forgive my curiosity. But tell me, didn't you live with Kaushika as his wife?'

Mahadevi looked pensive, but it seemed she did not mind the question.

'No,' she answered gravely. 'I know what you are asking. No. I only stayed in his palace for twenty-seven days, but not as his wife. You may say that I deceived him. I had no other way. He believed that sooner or later I would willingly become his wife. That of course would never have happened. He broke his promise and that made it easy for me to leave him.'

'And you walked away and have been on foot for nearly a month now! I can't believe this. But how do you manage without clothes? Forgive me if I sound rude, but...'

She paused, wondering if she was being too intrusive. Mahadevi didn't appear to be offended or troubled, she merely looked on, expecting her to finish.

'I mean,' Gowravva continued, 'how do you manage when you have your monthly periods?'

'Sister,' Mahadevi answered plainly, without any fuss, 'I stopped menstruating two years back.'

'That's very strange,' exclaimed Gowravva, 'it's not normal.'

'It's finished,' Mahadevi said simply with a smile.

Finished! The woman gaped at Mahadevi and then her eyes rolled and she looked lost in thought.

'You know,' she suddenly began, now growing nostalgic and her eyes becoming moist, 'one time I too had dreamt of a life like yours.' Then she wiped her eyes dry with the pallu of her sari, and started to tell her story.

'We are six sisters and I'm the youngest. Upset with my mother for not giving him a son, my father took another wife and, as his luck would have it, had another line of three daughters.' Gowravva laughed as if it was something funny, and then continued, 'It's all very strange. We desire for things that can never be fulfilled and when we think we have really fulfilled our desire, it turns out to be a curse! Imagine, I have six sons, not a single daughter I so much wanted to have. It is fate! It is all written in our fate the day we are born. There isn't much we can do about it.

'Looking back, I think I have just motioned through life without making any choice. I mean I have lived according to the choices made for me by others. But, as a little girl, I was very different. I was very keen and particular about my clothes, jewels, bangles, my hairdo and things like that. I was quite a fussy girl, and very stubborn, too. One day, we were all getting ready to go to a wedding and I wanted to wear a particular gold chain that belonged to my mother. She refused to give it to me, saying it would be too big for me and I would lose it. But I kicked up a row and to silence me, my mother branded me on my chin with a burning bangle.'

Gowravva showed a tiny scar on her chin and smiled wistfully. 'That marked the end of my little desires and fun. From that day I never demanded anything from my parents, or from anybody else for that matter. Something snapped inside me, and all those little things that at one time gave me great pleasure turned into pain. I thought my parents and sisters didn't love me and my feelings for them died. I wanted to leave home, but I didn't know where to go. Slowly, that desire too died out.'

Gowravva paused, pursing her lips, and then breaking into a little laugh, she said, 'O it all looks like a dream I had dreamt in my past life. Yes, when I was about twelve years old, this urge to leave home surfaced again. It was about that time I happened to see Mathe Yogeshwari. Mother Yogeshwari is no more; she passed away about ten years back. She was a yogini, a realised soul. When she came to our village, I went with my parents to see her. One look at me and she asked, "What is your name?" and then she said, "I can see that you are ripe enough to tread the spiritual path. What are you doing here, come with me." O, I so much wanted to run away with her; I was so desperate. I thought at last my desire to leave home, leave everything was going to be fulfilled.

But that was not to be. My parents of course didn't let me go with her; instead, they got me married.' Gowravva paused, giggling as if her past was all one long amusing story. 'I had six sons, every two years one, six sons and not a single daughter. But it was not in my hands, was it?'

'I have no regrets,' She sighed. 'I have done my duty as a wife and as a mother. All my sons are married and well settled. I think I have now really come to the end of this samsaric life. I wouldn't say I have lived a happy life, nor would I say a particularly sad one. I don't know. But still there is that little desire in me to live a life that'll be purely my own, without any encumbrances, totally free! Now I'm ready to leave.'

'You want to leave?' asked Mahadevi, not too surprised. 'But where to?'

'Can I come with you?'

Mahadevi studied the woman for a while with affectionate eyes. 'Sister,' she said, 'I don't know what to say. I have travelled alone all these days and I need no protection and desire no companion. I'll be going to Kalyana and from there I don't know where else to, or what I'll do.'

'No, not to protect you,' Gowravva reacted quickly, 'I know a woman of God like you needs no protection from mortals like me. I want to come because I too want to go to Kalyana with you. Somehow this one desire has remained with me, I have no other desire.'

'I'm not much of a friendly person,' warned Mahadevi.

'I don't expect anything,' said Gowravva. 'Maybe you are the godsend excuse for me to leave home. And I assure you, I wouldn't be a bother.'

'What about your husband?'

'He can come with me if he wants to,' said Gowravva calmly, and it seemed she had already thought over the matter. 'Or, he may live with our sons. My sons would of course miss me, but they'll learn. In any case, they have their own families to worry about.'

'You are remarkable!' said Mahadevi.

Gowravva laughed, shaking her head; then, looking into the eyes of Mahadevi, said, 'I'll tell you something. When I first saw you, the first thought that came to me was: who is this goddess? And then the image of Mathe Yogeshwari, with her long, curly hair, flashed through my mind. And it seems to me now that, without my knowing, I have been waiting for you. It's as if Mathe Yogeshwari has come back for me in your form. It's not a mere coincidence that you had to fall ill and come here.'

Somavva

A thick blanket of dark clouds spread across the sky, snuffing out the moon and her far relatives. Gusts of wind rose every so often and tore through the land like an army of wild beasts. Inside the hut, a lone oil lamp burned low, and it seemed a small congregation of ghosts were performing some strange ritual and, now and again, breaking into raucous mirth. In a corner sat Bahurupi and Nage, drinking toddy. Bahurupi seemed to be in a sad mood, swaying his body this way and that, and grunting. Was it because he had been away from his wife and son for too long, away from Kalyana, or was it because he had performed badly that evening and was feeling sick and low?

Nage kept grinning and chortling like a cock, which appeared to deepen Bahurupi's sorrow. Suddenly, it seemed to Bahurupi that there was something deeply impersonal about sorrow, something like the heavy wind outside that rose suddenly from nowhere and roared over the hut, threatening to bring it down.

'Don't get so serious,' chuckled Nage.

'What?' shouted Bahurupi over the din.

'You forget they are only stories. The reality is often very different and complex.'

'What do you mean? Are you saying that I'm telling lies, that I'm false?'

Nage grinned, delighted by Bahurupi's discomfiture. 'Brother, lies are only another form of stories, revealing yet another side to reality.'

'Nage, Nage,' said Bahurupi, getting very irritated, 'I would rather you stop philosophizing and stick to your jokes.'

'Jokes are funny stories with hidden philosophies.'

'You are impossible,' cried Bahurupi and broke into a laugh. 'All right, tell me, what is it you want to say?'

'Rather, I want to ask you a personal question?'

'Go ahead, my friend. Feel free,' said Bahurupi, smiling expansively now.

'You miss your wife, right?'

'Of course, I do. But is it so obvious?'

'Of course, it's also quite understandable. It's raining and you are feeling chilly and nostalgic. A perfectly romantic time to be at home with your wife.'

Bahurupi laughed, and looking Nage in the eye, asked, 'How about you, my friend? Haven't you ever felt the need for a woman?'

'I'm a woman,' said Nage, winking.

Bahurupi took a long draft of the toddy straight from the earthen pot, exhaled deeply and looked around as if to see if everything was going well with other drinkers. And then, sighing and glaring at Nage, said, 'Please, Nage, at least once be serious.'

'I'm always serious,' Nage replied (gravely), picked the toddy pot with his left hand, took a long sip, made a wry face and put it down. Wiping his mouth with the back of his hand, and tucking loose strands of hair behind his ears, he said rather pompously, 'You know something, I'm beyond sex.'

Bahurupi's eyebrows rose in surprise, and then laughing, he cried, 'Oh, Nage, Nage, don't fool yourself, man. Nobody is beyond sex. That reminds me of Narada's illusion! You know the story of Narada falling prey to sexual desire, to maya?'

'Ah! Strange are the ways of maya,' Bahurupi sang. 'Even gods are not spared from her insidious ways, not to speak of humorists and poor storytellers like you and me. Now listen to this story. Once, Narada, the earliest and pre-eminent among the storytellers of the three worlds, and our own beloved ancestor, fell into a trap, which was, of course, of his own making.

'One day, while on his itinerary, Narada made a brief stop at Kailasa to offer his greetings and respects to Shiva and Parvati. On entering the abode of Shiva, he saw the Lord, lying down with his head rested on Parvati's lap, while Parvati, playing with his matted hair, was singing some melodious tune. On seeing Narada barge in, Parvati moved away, blushing. Narada was embarrassed as he was upset. Yet he managed a smile and boastfully said, "Mother, you ought not to feel ashamed of my presence. You know I'm beyond body-mind dualism, beyond pleasure and pain, beyond desire and fear, beyond sex, beyond the reach of maya."

'"Even such a one should have the decency to knock on the door before you enter someone else's chamber," snapped Parvati.

'"But, mother," Narada protested, "I'm beyond even decency and indecency." Then he looked at Shiva and asked, 'And this is my home as well, isn't that so, my Lord?"

'Shiva laughed. "Yes," he mumbled, "the whole world is your home and all creatures including the gods are your characters!"

'"He is so stupidly presumptuous," cried Parvati in anger, "and you are encouraging him to wallow in that illusion."

'"Am I, Narada?" Shiva asked, winking at him.

'"Certainly not, my Lord," replied the poet-singer. "I'm truly blessed, at least you understand me!"

'"I can't stand this nonsense," Parvati flared up again and got up to leave.

'"No," pleaded Shiva, stopping her. And then turning to Narada, he said, "Parvati seems to be quite upset. Let's leave her alone for a while. Come on, you and I will go for a walk."

'Shiva took Narada by hand down to the earth. There, walking by a river, Shiva asked, 'Narada, isn't it time for your ablutions and prayer?"

'"Ah, yes," said Narada, nodding his head. "Living itself is an inescapable ritual." And leaving his famous tuneful lute on the bank, he stepped into the river. No sooner had Narada started washing himself than Shiva picked Narada's lute and vanished into thin air.

'Refreshed, Narada comes out of the water not as the eternal brahmachari, but transformed into a beautiful woman. Just then, a King, called Taladhwaja, comes that way. And lo, he instantly falls in love with her, marries her and makes her his queen. For twelve long years the king and the queen enjoy the pleasures of the body, losing all sense of time.

'The queen becomes pregnant eight times and brings forth eight sons. Several more years pass, the sons get married and soon the palace is bustling with children. The queen is very happy and she becomes happiness itself. But, one day, as fate would have it, the enemies attack the country and all her sons and grandsons are killed in the battle. Soon, the king too dies and the queen is left in great sorrow. Disillusioned with life, the queen decides to end her life and enters the river. But she doesn't die; rather, the queen is transformed back to Narada the man.'

No sooner had Bahurupi ended the story than Nage shouted, 'Bahurupi, you are a real cheat. This story is not from Shivapurana. You have stolen it from the Vaishnava tradition. You can't fool me, my friend.'

'Come on, Nage, don't be silly,' countered Bahurupi.

'We, storytellers, all steal. Nothing is our own.' Then throwing his arm over Nage's shoulder in an affectionate gesture, he continued, 'And you should know by now that there are only stories, stories of God and Creation, of human and God, of man and woman, of love and death; only names and language and location may change from period to period.'

'I know, I know,' Nage drawled, patting Bahurupi's arm. 'But, my friend, more fundamentally, this story of Narada points out that every person is both man and woman, a combination of both masculine and feminine qualities. So, in effect, quite unknowingly, you have told a story not to poke fun at me, but to endorse my view.'

'O, come on, Nage. The story clearly shows how even the gods are not beyond sexual desire, beyond samsara, let alone someone like you or me. So stop boasting and don't fall under the illusion like Narada.'

'You think you are too clever!'

'You think you are too intelligent!'

An hour later, after the rain stopped and the moon came out of the clouds like one seeking a warm sun in winter, Nage and Bahurupi, swaying this way and that, giggling and laughing, entered the dark lane of the town. Somavva was too happy to see the two friends and took them straight into her room. Bereft of her jewels, with the sacred ash mark on her forehead, clad in dark yellow cotton, she looked more a holy woman than a prostitute.

'I kept myself free for you both. Also, today is my day of prayer,' she gushed. 'O, I would have been sorely disappointed if you two hadn't come.'

'How could we not when a wise and virtuous one like you sends word. We are your slaves,' said Nage, teasingly.

'No need to flatter me,' said Somavva. She placed a bowl of fruits in front of them, then considering them with her big eyes, she started to laugh. 'Looks like you both are already high! I'll not offer you people any drink tonight,' she said. But when both, Nage and Bahurupi, made faces of disappointment. Somavva gave in. 'But on one condition that you'll both first listen to my new composition.'

'Of course, we're dying to hear it!' Bahurupi shouted, feigning interest.

'Another story in the making!' quipped Nage.

Somavva brought out a sheaf of palm leaves on which she had inscribed her vachanas. 'Now listen; don't sleep,' she said and then started to read.

> *Listen sister, listen brother,*
> *the eyes of the world are not to be trusted.*
> *When they see one with breasts and long hair,*
> *they call it woman;*
> *when they see one with moustache and beard,*
> *they call it man.*
> *But tell me, sister,*
> *what were we in our mother's womb?*
> *What is gender when the body*
> *is buried six feet deep?*
> *I am neither woman, nor man.*
> *I am a devotee of Nirlajjeshwara,*
> *the Lord Without Shame.*

Nodding his head in appreciation, Nage winked mischievously at Bahurupi.

'Somavva,' Bahurupi asked, 'is it your own composition?'

'That is what I said, my dear friend,' replied Somavva, looking a little hurt. 'But why do you ask?'

With some hesitation, Bahurupi said, 'There are already vachanas with more or less the same words or words to that effect by our Devara Dasimayya, Sankavva and Satyakka.'

'O, really,' cried Somavva with disbelief. 'I didn't know.'

'It doesn't matter, Somavva,' Nage interjected in her defence. 'This is your experience just as what the others have said was theirs.' And then with a mischievous gusto, he added, 'And, Somavva, this is my experience, too.'

While Bahurupi glared at Nage, Somavva, feeling somewhat comforted, laughed in good humour. Then getting quite excited, studying Bahurupi with her big eyes, Somavva said, 'Bahurupi, chant some vachanas from our women poets. I'm curious to know. I really am.'

'Yes, yes, let's listen to the voice of the wise one,' shouted Nage. Frowning, smiling, and then with a little laugh, Bahurupi nodded and shut his eyes for a while to better recall the vachanas he had not used for quite some time now. 'O yes,' he said, opening his eyes, and chuckling, as if recalling some pleasant memory; then he coughed, as if to clear his throat, folded his arms across his chest, and said, 'This one is Sankavva,' and then chanted:

> *All their talk of Shiva comes to a pause*
> *at the feet of young women...*
> *There is no difference*
> *between Kailasa and the world...*
> *Woman is not maya*
> *but an aspect of God.*

Her back erect, legs folded, Somavva sat on a divan, listening, nodding, eyes moist with tears.

> *Born on earth in a man's world,*
> *trapped in karma*
> *and drowned in samsara,*
> *I was immersed in darkness.*

> *My mother tied a husband to my neck,*
> *Father Jangama blessed me with a linga, and lo,*
> *the darkness burst into light,*
> *karma dissolved, mind went empty,*
> *I was free...*

'That was Lingamma for you,' said Bahurupi and then recited a few more vachanas. Somavva did not speak for a long while. Then slowly, as one coming out of a daze, she shook her head, wiped the tears with the loose end of her sari. 'How foolish of me,' she said, 'to think I'm the only miserable one, struggling through this muck of life.'

The two friends darted a glance at each other but did not say anything. Somavva smiled, feeling somewhat embarrassed. Studying her, Bahurupi tried to imagine her dressed in silk and jewels for her wealthy customers. But now, even in plain yellow sari and without jewels, with her large eyes and sensuous lips and ample bossoms, she looked seductive! Any man would lose his heart and throw away a fortune to have her, he thought.

They remained silent, all three, as if suddenly words had lost their meaning. The sky rumbled somewhere faraway, gusts of cold air swept through the window and ruffled Somavva's fine, silky hair. And then the rain started to fall in big drops, and the air inside the room turned cool and pleasant. Slowly, hesitantly, breaking the silence, Nage said, 'In a few days we both will be leaving to Kalyana. Why don't you join us?'

'O, you are so kind,' said Somavva quickly, shaking her head. 'But I have to finish a few things here before I go anywhere.' Then, overcome with feelings, her eyes going moist again, she said, 'You two are great. What can I offer you both? I want to make you both happy.'

Feeling awkward and deeply ashamed of his lustful thoughts a while ago, Bahurupi avoided her eyes and pretended to be excited by the offer. 'Yes,' he cried, 'bring out the drink you have hidden away in your cupboard.'

'Yes, we are thirsty,' agreed Nage, a wide grin on his face.

As the two friends, now chatting and laughing, started to drink from the silver cups, Somavva sat in front of them, her bosom swelling with feelings she could not define nor express.

'Somavva,' Nage asked, gazing at her with kindly eyes, 'can I ask you a personal question?'

'Brother, my life is like an open field.'

'Tell us your story,' said Nage, putting the cup down.

'Yes, yes, I'm all ears,' Bahurupi nodded, taking another greedy sip from his cup.

Sniffing back her tears and after much shaking of her head and much hesitation, Somavva told them her story.

'My mother was a prostitute in the town of Nagevadi. I'm her second daughter. One night, my elder sister ran away with a man who regularly visited my mother; she must have been about fifteen or sixteen years old at that time. We don't know if she willingly went with him, or she was forcefully taken away by the man. There has been no trace of her so far. After her going away, my mother became quite possessive and fiercely protective of me. She wouldn't let me go out with my friends or go out even to the bazaar. I don't know what went wrong with my mother, she died a year after my sister's leaving. She had been seriously ill for quite some time and didn't reveal it to anybody, or my sister's going away affected her badly, I'm not too sure. She took to bed and refused to see anyone. One night, when I took her the medicines the vaidya had given, she had turned cold and stiff, with a linga clutched in her right hand.'

'Shiva-linga!' Bahurupi looked extremely amused. 'Was she a Shiva bhakte?'

'I don't know,' said Somavva. 'I don't remember her ever worshipping Shiva. I think the man who visited her last probably gave her the linga. She never went out, so there is no other way she would have come to possess that linga. Three months before her death, that night—after which she never saw anyone again—I saw the man just as he was leaving my mother's room. He was a strange looking man with a long beard and long hair that came down to almost his waist. In the dark I couldn't see his face, of course. But later, when I asked her about the man, she refused to say anything.'

Bahurupi and Nage glanced at each other but did not say anything, nor did they express any surprise at this apparently curious twist in the story.

'Anyway,' continued Somavva, with a distant look in her eyes, 'it is that sacred linga which I preserved and began to worship that has made me what I'm today.'

'Do you have children, Somavva?' Nage asked without warning.

And Somavva, in spite of herself, burst into little giggles. 'No, no,' she said. 'But, I must tell you this. Once, two years ago, a young man wanted me to be his mistress and give him a child. I think he was a fairly wealthy man. He was married for five years without a child. He said he was fond of children but God had not been kind to him. He even offered to marry me.'

'And what did you say?' asked Nage.

'Oh, brother, you must know that in my profession I have seen all kinds of men. Young men, middle-aged men, religious men, business people, travellers, even old men who couldn't stand steadily on their feet. There were some who wanted me to be their mistress, some who treated me as if I were a piece of rotten fruit, yet wanted me to do crazy things to them. Men who would remove their sacred threads, their linga, or wipe the vermilion mark or ash mark from their foreheads before touching me. And men, who, after the act, would grab my feet and sob like little kids. Oh, all kinds of men! And I tell you, sometimes it was such great fun, just as at other times, it used to be sheer pain and unbearable agony. I have seen and experienced life not merely in my mind and heart, but in the very marrow of my bones. But I know it is a ridiculous life I live, it is not the life I want, it is only business. I really want to finish with this, leave everything and go to Kalyana and meet Basavanna. But I have a few unfinished tasks that I need to complete. The time is not far, and I'll be ready when it comes.'

Bahurupi's Dilemma

After nearly two years of giving performances in a number of towns and many villages, Bahurupi and Nage decided to break their journey and return to Kalyana. Allama and Siddarama were coming to Kalyana, and Bahurupi did not want to miss this rare opportunity to see and meet with Allama in his own hometown. Also, Bahurupi had grown weary of his storytelling and had begun to feel homesick. On their way back, much to Nage's consternation, he had continually chattered about his family.

'O how will my son look now? Wouldn't he have grown tall? And my wife! Ah, I really can't wait to see them...'

'It's like describing the taste of food before you have eaten,' Nage remarked irritably.

'You don't have a family,' Bahurupi snapped back rather unkindly, 'and you have no way of understanding my emotions.'

It was indeed, for Bahurupi, an emotional reunion with his family. His five-year old son had grown tall and pretty. Gathering his son in his arms, he broke into tears of joy. But when his wife emerged from her room, carrying a dark-skinned, gurgling baby, he felt the ground under him sinking, and all his joy of returning home turned dark and bitter.

He looked shattered when he met Nage that evening by the Tripuranthaka Lake. They squatted by the lake and talked late into the night. 'How could she do this to me? How could she?' Bahurupi kept repeating and crying unashamedly.

'What is your problem?' asked Nage.

'The baby is not mine. I know it. I should know. And you still ask what my problem is?'

'But how sure are you? It could be yours? Did you speak to her? Did *she* say it is not your child?'

Bahurupi did not answer. People, who had come into the town on business or to meet their relatives, were frantically moving up and down the lake, looking for boats that would take them back home. The sun was on the other side of the town, and the lake was turning dark brown.

'All right, what do you want to do now?' asked Nage. 'Find the lover and kill him, kill your wife, and strangle the baby because you think it is not yours?'

'Yes,' roared Bahurupi. 'That is exactly what I feel.'

'Then go and finish them all. Why are you sitting here, crying your heart out like a little boy? Go on and finish the job; I'm with you.'

Bahurupi couldn't belive his ears, he looked at his friend in the dying light, wondering why he was giving him such horrible advice. And of all people the ever jovial and wise Nage?

'You are a coward,' Nage said slowly, adding insult to injury.

'Shut up,' yelled Bahurupi, shaking with rage. 'You want to turn me into a killer? What kind of a friend are you?'

'What do you think?' asked Nage, provoking him further.

'I think you have gone insane,' cried Bahurupi. 'You think I hate my wife so much as to kill her? Or you think I'm some bloodthirsty killer who will not hesitate to butcher even a baby?'

'What then is your problem?' asked Nage, now deliberately raising his voice.

Bahurupi did not respond. He sat staring at the lake swallowing up the last rays of the sun and swelling in darkness. Suddenly the lake looked like an inverted sky, and the boats, plying on the lake, glimmering like moving stars.

Turning to his friend and in a voice quivering with despair, Bahurupi asked, 'Nage, my friend, tell me, what should I do now?'

Nage was harsh and pitiless.

'I have heard you say many times that you are either thinking and worrying about your wife, or thinking about Allama. You can stop worrying about your wife, now that you know she can manage her life even without you.'

'What are you saying?' Bahurupi screamed. 'Are you saying that I should ignore what has happened and continue to live with my wife, or that I must leave her?'

'Don't ask me,' replied Nage, now getting really irritated. 'It's your life, your problem. Solve it the best way you can. The other way, if there is one, is not to think of it as a problem at all. That is the way of life. All values are relative. Yours are not necessarily the best ones.'

Bahurupi held his head in his hands. A long time passed in silence and then, as if it was too agonizing for him to speak, he looked and pleaded, 'Nage, Nage, I don't know. I really can't think of anything right now. You talk, say something, but please don't tease me, don't hurt me. Nage, my friend, tell me a story.'

'A story for a storyteller, eh?' Laughed Nage and began promptly, as if he had only been waiting to be asked.

'I'll tell you not one but three stories. You know, according to tradition, you have to tell three stories, sing three songs, and give three discourses. That is the rule. You know why? Because one will not quench your thirst, two will not clear your doubts. And three will not satisfy you either; rather, it'll only confuse and confound you further and deepen your agony so much that you'll stop asking questions. In any case, my friend, no question can be answered to your satisfaction. So, why not do things three times over, just to keep ourselves going?'

'I'm listening,' said Bahurupi.

'Once upon a time there lived a famous couple. They did everything together and could not bear to be separated from each other even for a moment. Fearing that children would come in the way of their love, they even chose not to have children. Such was their love for each other. They lived and grew old in love, keeping constant company of each other through thick and thin of life. One day the wife died, as humans have to die one day or the other, either of illness or of old age or of some other cause. A day later, unable to bear the loss of his wife, the man too breathed his last and went to heaven. In heaven, he desperately wanted to meet his wife. He ran up and down, looking for her everywhere. At last, he found her sitting alone on a rock by a murmuring, celestial river, and humming a song to herself. Calling out her name, with outstretched arms, he rushed towards her. The woman turned, and looked scared. As he came and stopped in front of her, she looked up and asked frowningly, "Who are you?"

'The man gushed, "My dear girl, it is me, your dear husband."

'"What nonsense," she scowled. "I don't have any husband and I don't know who you are. You really scared the life out of me. Now please leave me alone."

Bahurupi gave a long sigh as if to say: All right, now move on to the next one.

'I can see that you are not serious enough to laugh,' Nage chortled. 'No problem, now listen to this tale and there is no need to laugh at this one either. Once, a young seeker, who was quite dissatisfied with the knowledge he had acquired from gurus and books, decided to carry out his own search to find the secret of life. His wife, who was devoted to him and also a seeker after truth in her own right, let him go without making any fuss and even wished him luck in his lofty endeavour. After long and vigorous tapas in the forest, the man came back, wearing long hair and a long beard and bright shining eyes, and smiling like one who had conquered the world. Happy to see him back, the wife cooked a special meal. As he ate his favourite dishes with great relish, she sat by him, admiring his huge beard and sparkling eyes, and speaking generally about the changes that had come over the village while he had been away. Only after the meal, she asked, "My dear husband, now tell me, did you find what you went looking for?"

'The man laughed gently and said, "Yes, my dear. I have found the truth. Your good wishes have borne fruit. I'm so lucky to have you as my wife."

'"What is this truth you have found, my dear?" asked the wife, with genuine curiosity.

'"Ah! It is difficult to explain," said the man. "Words cannot convey this truth. It is truly indescribable, beyond words. Still, if I have to use words to give you some sense of this truth, I would say that there is only one truth, one God, one life. Outwardly the expression of life may appear to be varied and different, but actually it is all same, everything is one reality, there is only one life. Our sense of separation, division or difference, is only an illusion." He paused suddenly as though he had used too many words, and then he asked his wife, "Did you understand what I said, my dear?"

'"I don't know," said the woman. "I'm trying..."

'"You see," continued the man, now overcome with enthusiasm to make her understand, "there is no separateness at all. No time, no space, no death, no birth. Everything is one and that is the Supreme Reality, the Ultimate Truth."

'"Well," responded the woman, now nodding her head and smiling timidly. "While you were away, I too have found something which I consider to be the truth, or at least one of the truths of life."

'The man started to laugh, but quickly controlled himself with the power of his will and then smiling gently, almost affectionately, asked, "What could that be, my dear?"

'"There is nothing permanent," declared the woman, emphasising the word "nothing". "Everything comes and goes, goes and comes in a never-ending cycle. To cling to something is to be attached to the memory of the past that is already dead and gone."

"Interesting discovery," murmured the man, his eyes growing wide with surprise at the new avatar of his wife.

'"You see," continued the woman in the same even tone, "I discovered this fact while you were away and when I took a lover."

'As if struck by lightning the man fell silent, but his face contorted with inexpressible anguish. And then all of a sudden, his face flushed in rage, he exploded: "You took a lover? You betrayed me, betrayed your husband? O, what a cheat you turned out to be! Shameless whore!"

'"Stop it," cried the woman, raising her hand in a gesture of warning. "You of all people should not speak like that. Didn't you say that our sense of separation is all wrong, that all is one? And that there is only one life, one Supreme Reality, and everything else is an illusion? And didn't I say that there is nothing permanent, not even the relationship between husband and wife? Where then is the question of betrayal here? I'm telling you the truth…"

Bahurupi sighed and chuckled, the chuckle soon cracking into a loud laughter, and then the laughter into uncontrollable sobs.

The moon was on the lake, and the lake, with no boats plying now, was quiet like a man in deep contemplation.

'I have not told you the third and last one yet,' shouted Nage. 'Now stop your laughing and crying and listen attentively. This is not a story. This is the end of all stories.' And he chanted:

> *I saw the corpse of samsara*
> *alive with swarming worms.*
> *I saw dogs come to devour*
> *the reeking body, start a fight.*
> *But I didn't see you anywhere there,*
> *O Lord Guheshvara.*

'Allama...,' mumbled Bahurupi, wiping the tears with the back of his hand.

'Yes, Bahurupi. I know you recited it in your last performance. You have memorized these vachanas well. But, what does it mean?'

When Bahurupi stood up, the moon had climbed to the centre of the sky and there was dead silence all round. 'I should go now,' he said heavily. 'My wife will have cooked a special meal tonight.'

'Aha!' said Nage. 'But wouldn't you want to invite your friend to partake of this special meal with your family?'

'No,' replied Bahurupi, and the next moment he was gone, like the moon behind a mass of clouds.

Kalyana

Standing before the Mahamane, studying the massive structure and its architectural features, Allama remarked, 'Your Basavanna lives well and in style!'

The middle-aged, bearded sarana, Hadapada Appanna, who was at the door, saw the two strangers and quickly came over and greeted them with folded hands.

'We have come to meet Basavanna,' Siddarama said.

In his long ochre robe and ash mark on his forehead, Siddarama looked a jangama. But Allama, in a coarse top and wrinkled dhoti, long, unkempt hair and shaggy beard, impressed Appanna. He looks a yogi, Appanna thought. But it did not matter who they were. They were new to the place and had to be treated as guests. Appanna was courteous to a fault. With an amiable smile and hands joined in greeting and bending low, he welcomed them. 'Please come in and rest for a while. Anna is in puja, he'll join you soon.'

'We can't wait,' said Allama, impatiently.

Appanna rushed into the house and found Basava, sitting cross-legged before the Shiva-Linga, immersed in prayer. Generally no one dared disturb Basavanna during his prayers, not even his wives, but this seemed an extraordinary situation. Appanna stepped hesitantly into the puja room and whispered, 'Two jangamas are waiting to meet you.'

Basava nodded his head almost impercebtibly, but did not get up. Appanna came out and told the jangamas that Basava was just about to finish his puja, and invited them again most courteously to come inside and be seated.

Allama flew into a rage.

'Go and tell your Basava that we'll not step inside the house of a fake bhakta like him.' And then turning to Siddarama, he yelled, 'Come on, Siddarama, let's go.'

Before Appanna could react, the two visitors had turned their backs on him. So the one in ochre robe is Siddarama, gathered Appanna. But who is the other one? Allama Prabhu! Appanna had not seen Allama nor for that matter Siddarama before. Convinced now that the bearded one could be none other than the incomparable Prabhudeva, he raced back into the house to warn Basava. Soon, a barechested Basava, his forehead and arms smeared with holy ash, followed by Chenna Basava, Kinari Bommanna and boatman Chowdayya, rushed out looking for Allama and Siddarama. But the two men were nowhere near the house and Basava's heart skipped a beat. And then he saw, some distance away, two figures sitting at the foot of a spreading pipal tree.

With his bemused entourage at his heels, Basava rushed to the spot with folded palms.

'Forgive me, forgive me, I'm at fault,' he pleaded, almost bending double. 'Kindly excuse my fault and accept our hospitality.'

With a slight turn of his head and frowning, Allama looked up at Basava. 'You think your puja is more important and that we are nothing? You say a sarana is equal to Shiva in the flesh and yet this is the way you treat us? Your devotion is all a mere show. You think I'm going to be impressed by all this drama?'

'Prabhu,' Basava implored, in a trembling voice, 'you are our Shiva. I admit I erred. You must please forgive me.'

'Prabhudeva,' Chenna Basava said, stepping forward with palms together, 'we have been actually waiting for your arrival for the last two days.' The two elderly saranas,

Bommanna and Chowdayya, too, put their hands together in reverence, nodding their heads in agreement.

Allama stared at Chenna Basava. In his long hair and earrings and cleft chin, he looked the picture of a young Basava. 'Who are you?' Allama asked.

'My sister's son, Chenna Basava,' Basava intervened.

'A budding chief of your army, eh?' chuckled Allama, considering the young sarana not without admiration. Then turning to Basava, in a show of great annoyance, he asked, 'So, what is it that you want? Now put down your hands, I don't need this reverence; in fact, I detest any show of reverence.'

'We are truly blessed by your visit,' Basava said, his joined palms still held up in respect. 'You are our guru…'

'I'm nobody's guru,' said Allama, with an impatient wave of his hand. 'You are the guru, not me.' He laughed, like a sudden shower in summer; then turning to Siddarama, with a twinkle in his eye, he said, 'What do you say, Siddarama? Have you ever met bhaktas so simple, humble and wise? Aren't you happy coming here?'

Siddarama, who had held himself back all this while, sprang to his feet and took Basava's hands in his.

'For years I have wanted to come and meet you,' he said smiling. And then pressing Basava's hands affectionately, he gushed, 'I'm so happy I came here with Allama.'

'Saranas like you have been my inspiration,' Basava replied humbly.

Allama too stood up, caressing his beard and looking around with a frown on his face. 'It's so hot over here,' he said. 'Let's go in.'

'Whatever you say, you are our commander-in-chief,' quipped Siddarama, winking at Basava and breaking into a good-humoured laugh. And Basava led the way into the Great

Mansion that held several rooms for travelling jangamas and visitors.

Behind the Great Mansion was another large, recently put up structure, *Anubhava Mantapa*, the Hall of Experience. In the evenings, the saranas gathered there to share their experiences, their many doubts and conflicts, and debate over spiritual matters. Sometimes vachanas of the old masters and also newly composed ones by saranas were recited and discussed. A scribe maintained a record of these meetings. If not for these records, hundreds of vachanas would have been lost to future generations. For not all vachanakaras maintained written records of their compositions. From time to time, visiting jangamas and spiritual seekers from outside too were invited to these gatherings to share their experiences and speak to the saranas. In these meetings, Basava generally kept himself in the background and spoke only when he was pressed to speak, or when he felt compelled to intervene. There was no bar on caste or gender here. Women and men participated as equals and spoke freely.

That evening, Basava proposed that Allama should preside over their meeting at the Hall of Experience.

'You know I'm not good at these things,' Allama said. 'You should do it, Basava. You are the chosen one; it's your job, not mine.'

Allama had never given a discourse, nor had he presided over any such meetings before.

'For several months now,' implored Basava, 'we have been waiting for you to come and lead these discussions.'

As if amused, Allama laughed, caressed his beard, his eyes squinted.

'Basava,' Allama said with a grave face, 'I don't have a path I can call my own, much less a path to recommend to others. In fact, there is no such thing as a path to Reality;

rather, there is no path whatsoever to reach, to understand, to come upon this supreme understanding!'

'Now you see,' cried Basava, 'only you can say such things. You know, you have seen it all. So you should lead us and enlighten us on this pathless path.'

Shaking his head, Allama warned, 'Basava, don't do this. I may lead you nowhere, or only lead you to the edge of a precipice.'

Siddarama, who was listening to this curious conversation, guffawed, 'Basava, be warned! It'll be like inviting a lion into your household!'

'We are prepared,' declared Basava, and then joining his palms reverentially, he said, 'Throw us into water, throw us into fire, throw us down the precipice, do what you will with us. Your words will be our command.'

Allama sighed. 'You leave me with no choice, if this is the way you want to use me, so be it.'

'You could be a little more compassionate,' commented Siddarama, with a short laugh, indicating he was only joking. Saranas in Kalyana, including Basava, had hitherto only heard about Allama and formed ideas about him as a little weird but a great master. But, travelling with him for the last ten days, Siddarama knew that Allama did not care to please or be good to anyone, nor did he expect anyone to be nice to him. He did not care for sentiments and detested any show of goodness, though he could be extremely affable and as compassionate as a mother to a child. But you could never tell how he would respond to a particular situation or person. Siddarama knew that too well by now. One night, during their journey, just before going to sleep, he had asked of Allama, 'What is your interest in Kalyana?'

'I have no particular interest in anything or anyone,' Allama had answered, with some irritation. 'You think I was interested in you and so came to your place? It's just that you happened to be there in my path.'

'And what is this path of yours?' Siddarama had persisted.

'Tomorrow, I suppose we have to travel east to reach Kalyana. That is the only path.'

The Throne of Void

Clad in a new white silk top and silk dhoti—both of which had been offered to him by Basava—and in his long, shaggy beard, Allama looked a picture of an old man desperately trying to look like a bridegroom. He was of course never particular of the kind of dress he wore; whatever came his way, he just put them on. Sometimes he did wear ochre robes. Like food, clothes too were offered to him by bhaktas and he accepted them without demur. But he carried no spare clothes. He carried nothing, no pitcher, no stick, and no symbol of any spiritual tradition. He only carried himself tall and straight, and spoke directly as thoughts came to him. He never spoke just to talk; rather he spoke without thinking and never thought over what he spoke. He was like a river, and as it is in the nature of a river to flow, he went wherever his feet took him. He had no destination in mind, whichever place he halted became his destination.

In his new, shining clothes, when he stepped into the Anubhava Mantapa, followed by Basava, Chenna Basava, and boatman Chowdayya, the nearly five hundred saranas stood up with respect and greeted him in one voice. The hall was built like an indoor theatre. At one end was a raised platform and around it, in the shape of a horseshoe, seats had been built of bricks and mortar. And there were six entrances, symbolising the six phases of the faith.

In the middle of the dais, a large seat called *Sunya Simhasana*, Throne of Void, looked majestic, like a king's throne, with inlaid gold. Allama took the seat, unsmiling, looking quite severe. On both sides of the throne were smaller seats on which sat Basava, Chenna Basava, Chowdayya, and

Siddarama. Down below on the left, women sat together in a row. The two wives of Basava, Neela and Ganga, were seated in the front row, their foreheads marked with holy ash. On the men's side, in the back row, sat Bahurupi and Nage, eagerly waiting for Allama to speak.

The first round of discussion centred on Allama. The saranas were very curious to know all about Allama's background: his parents, his guru, his sadhana and experiences. They wanted to know if he was really married, if so, what happened to his wife. They wanted to know if it was true that he accidentally discovered a cave and that inside the cave, he met a yogi and received diksha from him. And then they were keen to know of his understanding of kayaka, linga, and anubhaava.

But Allama refused to answer questions about his life. They were of no importance to anybody, he said dismissively. And with regard to anubhaava, kayaka and linga, he said that Basava and Siddarama were the right people to explain them.

'Prabhu,' Siddarama said, reacting to Allama's indifference and curt refusal to answer questions, 'be kind enough to answer the questions. Saranas are very eager and anxious to hear your story from your own mouth. If you do not answer, they'll continue to believe in the stories already circulating about you. And you must know that there are all kinds of stories about you. One may not know which to believe and which not to. There is one in which your birth was a divine one, that you were found in the Shiva temple of Balligave, and that your father and mother were only foster parents. According to another one, you are supposed to be an incarnation of Lord Shiva and you are here to destroy adharma and to awaken people to their spiritual consciousness. There is also a weird one which says that you are not the real one, but only an apparition of the real one who is in an unknown cave of the Himalayas. Also, some people believe...'

'Enough,' shouted Allama, raising his hand. 'This is nothing but a figment of someone's rich imagination.' Then turning to the saranas, he said, 'Don't believe in all these weird stories. There is nothing extraordinary about my birth and growing up. It is like anybody else's. Don't attribute any divine purpose to my birth. Better still to believe that every birth is divine, even the birth of a buffalo, a dog, or a bedbug.

'If this be the truth, then, what is so special about my birth? Nothing whatsoever, right? There is no special story to tell here. Like everyone else I was born of a woman. And like an idiot I too went in search of God, struggled through all kinds of sadhana. There is nothing I did not try, including sleeping with a corpse and eating from a skull and doing tapas standing on one leg. And then there came a point when I felt totally disgusted with myself and my search for things that existed only in my imagination. The very will to search, to do anything, even the urge to quench my thirst and hunger, broke down. Everything came to a standstill, to a nought, and I found myself free. I don't know how it happened and therefore, I have no way of talking about it.'

Siddarama smiled to himself. He had hoped that Allama would give the saranas details of his life and clarify their doubts, removing their confusion. But all that Allama was giving them was a string of puzzles. More conundrums to chew upon! No signs, no direction, no path. Siddarama turned to Basava expecting him to intervene. But Basava only smiled back as if to say, 'Yes, I wonder, too.'

A daring sarana stood up and asked rather bluntly, 'Prabhu, were you married?'

Caressing his beard, grinning mischievously, Allama replied, 'Yes, I was married. And my wife died of illness after three months of our marriage. It was good she died early, otherwise, married to one like me, she would have died of misery, or who knows, she might even have committed suicide.'

The saranas were stunned by Allama's apparently crude, insensitive answer. Was there a message in his crude replies? Or, was he just trying to impress them that he was above and beyond the ordinary. However, another sarana now got up and asked, 'Prabhu, in one of your early vachanas, you mention Animishayya, the one without eyelids. Was he the yogi you met inside a cave?'

Grinning wickedly, Allama replied, 'I didn't meet any yogi without eyelids or without eyes, either inside the cave or outside. I don't know who gave you that vachana or where you heard it. It must surely be a product of someone's imagination.'

'No, it's in your vachana,' the sarana insisted. 'And you do mention Animishayya.'

'Then, it could be my imagination. There is nothing more to it. Now forget about it. It has no significance whatsoever.'

Murmurs of disappointment burst from the crowd, like bubbles on a lake. Allama was dismissing their questions rather than answering them. He was harsh and snappy and appeared to be angry about something. But why? The saranas looked at Basava willing him to intervene. But it was Chenna Basava who stood up.

'Prabhu,' he folded his palms in respect and asked, 'what does "Animishayya" mean?'

'Open-eyed one.'

'What does it mean?'

'When there is no thought, then your eyes don't blink, they stay open, that's what it means.'

'I don't understand.'

'When *you* are not there, you'll know.'

Chenna Basava couldn't figure out what Allama implied.

'I have another question,' he said quickly. 'Almost all your vachanas end with a reference to Lord Guhesvara. What or who is Guhesvara?'

'Good question,' chuckled Allama. 'It's not what you think: Lord of caves like Lord of rivers, Lord of the sky, Lord of the heart or what have you. It only means the hidden one, the mystery, the unknown.'

'You mean the Supreme Reality, the Infinite Absolute, is hidden, unknown?'

'Mere words.'

'But words that work as signs, guiding symbols, aren't they?'

'Listen,' shouted Allama, quite irritated now. 'When there is no outside or inside, when there is no I or other, where is the sign, where is the need for any sign or symbol?'

'Yes, Prabhu,' Chenna Basava agreed humbly, tactfully. 'But, we can approach or understand that only through symbols, is it not?'

'Ah! You are clever!' Allama sighed. 'This talking is not going to help. Language only destroys.'

'You mean language destroys meaning?'

'It only means language fragments and distorts reality and thereby falsifies your understanding.'

'What then is real understanding?' demanded Chenna Basava.

Allama said:

> *The one who knows joy is not the happy one,*
> *the one who knows sorrow is not the unhappy one,*
> *the one who knows both joy and sorrow*
> *is not the jnani, only the one who grasps*

*the sign of the dead and
of the one who was never born,
knows Lord Guhesvara.*

Chenna Basava flushed. What is the sign of the dead and the unborn one? Confused and at a loss for words, he slid back, pondering over what seemed to be Allama's new vachana.

Basava turned to see if Ganadeva, the scribe, who was sitting close to the dais before a desk, was recording the dialogue or was lost in listening to it.

Inspired by Allama's utterances, —which would be converted into vachanas years later—Moligayya, an elderly sarana, almost half-bent with age and illness, rose with difficulty from his seat. But his voice, loud and deep, belied his frail body.

'Have you seen an infant die before its birth?' he asked. 'Or, born before its death? Between the two, tell me, who is the one born before death, and the one who dies before birth? Not understanding the two and that which is in between, what can I say of those caught up in delusion?'

The crowd came alive. Springing to his feet, a much-inspired Machayya shouted, 'Wonderful! Wonderful!! What is that that is in between? Brilliant! In effect, Moligayya, you have asked the most important question. And, if I could put it a little differently, what is the relationship between a bhakta and God? Sometimes I feel I know, sometimes I get very confused. Be that as it may, I remember a vachana of Prabhudeva on this subject. It goes like this:

*Like the presence in an idol,
reflection in water,
tree in a seed,
silence in sound
is your relationship with saranas,
O Lord Guhesvara.*

Having recited the vachana, Machayya asked of Allama, 'What exactly does it mean, Prabhudeva?'

'Why do you ask?' Allama countered, frowning. 'Isn't the answer there in the vachana itself? But then that is no real answer.' And he burst out laughing at his own wit. Then calming down, he continued, 'It is like a treasure hidden in the earth, like lightning hidden in the dark clouds, like light in your eyes; but you'll never know.'

A long time passed in silence. It was the silence between words, between sounds, and it was unnerving. Ganadeva, who had been immersed in writing, lifted his head, wondering why no one was speaking. Allama, who was now surveying the gathering, noticed Bahurupi in the back row and yelled out like one hollering to someone across a stream, 'O, you are there, the clever storyteller!'

Adjusting his orange colour turban and blushing, Bahurupi stood up and put his palms together in reverence.

'It seems to me that you are all more interested in stories,' Allama said pointing at Bahurupi, and addressing the gathering in general. 'You should ask him; he is the one who can tell you stories.'

Many heads turned to Bahurupi, some sniggered, some frowned, while a few wondered why Allama was changing the course of what was becoming a very enlightening discussion. Finding his opportunity to speak, a beaming Bahurupi said, 'Prabhu, you are the story that has no beginning, no middle and no end.'

'So are you, friend,' bellowed Allama, 'so is everyone.'

'I do not know about that,' Bahurupi said, raising his voice. 'But, Prabhu, what I know is that all of us start our lives with stories. We come to know and begin to understand the world around us and ourselves through stories—stories of life and death, of joy and sorrow; stories of love, hatred, jealousy, pride, devotion and all that. There simply is no end.

Or, perhaps one could say that the end is in the beginning, and beginning in the end. But, still, it's a mystery. It remains a mystery. What is this mystery, Prabhu?'

'What is your name?' asked Allama.

The smile on Bahurupi's face faded. 'Bahurupi Chowdayya,' he replied, wondering if Allama had really forgotten his name or was just teasing him.

'You are that mystery, Bahurupi Chowdayya!'

'If I'm that mystery,' continued Bahurupi, now smiling and quite excited, 'does it mean that if I know myself, I'll understand that mystery?'

'If you can really know yourself, if your eyes can really see themselves, you may.'

'Prabhu, I can see myself in the mirror; my eyes can see themselves in the mirror!'

'Good answer! Brilliant!! Excellent!!!' shouted several saranas.

'Do you, really?' asked Allama. 'Do you see yourself or do you see only the idea or image of yourself? If you can see yourself without the idea, without the image of what or who you are, you'll be fortunate. Try it.'

Silenced, Bahurupi sat down, thinking about Allama's remark. Again, a disconcerting silence descended on the hall. Siddarama sighed, Basava smiled, and Ganadeva wrote furiously. Having finished his notes, Ganadeva dropped his pen on the desk and stood up. 'Prabhudeva, I have a question,' he said, surprising everyone.

'There is no answer,' said Allama, now looking annoyed.

'But I can't help asking, Prabhu,' pleaded Ganadeva.

'Then just ask and be done with it.'

'In one of your vachanas you say Lord Brahma and Lord Vishnu burn to ashes, elsewhere you say Ganga and

Gowri become widows. And you even refer to the linga dying in your palm. What do you mean by these expressions? I'm intrigued.'

'Do you want to write your commentaries on those lines?' Allama asked rudely. 'What do you want to know?'

'I just want to know what those terrible lines mean.'

'You'll know when you burn all those silly notes you are taking down,' roared Allama and he stood up, indicating the meeting was over.

But no one got up, except Nage, who in his long hair and long gown, sprang to his feet with his hand raised, drawing the attention of Allama.

'What is it? What do you want?' shouted Allama.

'You don't seem to approve of anything,' Nage said. 'You find fault with everything and reject everything. Why then do you travel so much and why do you speak at all? More importantly, why are you here?'

Sounds of both disapproval and appreciation rose from the crowd. It was indeed a relevant yet tricky question.

'I travel and speak,' Allama answered, 'because I have nothing better to do and because I can't help it.'

He stared at Nage for a long moment, smiling into his beard. The saranas held their breath, wondering what Allama would say next. Raising his hand and raising his voice, Allama said, 'You think you are very smart, eh? Will you ask a bird why it sings and why it keeps flying from place to place? Will you?' and then with a sudden wave of his hand as if to say all questions are silly, he started to move down the dais.

❖ ❖ ❖

Challenging Allama

The next day, the Hall of Experience was bulging at the seams. With no seats untaken several saranas either squatted or stood wherever they could find a little space. An air of great expectancy hung in the hall, like hunger before a meal. When Chenna Basava, clad in a long silk robe, stood large on the dais and challenged Allama to answer his questions, saranas sat in utter silence, admiring his courage and tact.

Chenna Basava commanded the respect of even the senior saranas twice his age. In his late twenties, with prominent nose, big eyes and cleft chin, he looked almost a replica of young Basavanna, and had even his mannerisms. But unlike Basava, he was no soft-spoken gentleman with a melting heart. He was tough, aggressive and very practical in his dealings with the saranas. When he spoke, he spoke to the point, and saranas listened to him with great interest and admiration. His wide reading, rigorous discipline and unwavering devotion humbled and inspired many a sarana.

Chenna Basava first offered his pranams to Allama and then, with renewed vigour and determination, began.

'Prabhu, I do not understand why you reject the need for bhakti. Don't you think that without bhakti we'll be lost in the hustle and bustle of samsara? Bhakti is certainly not the end but a means to the end. Bhakti is the boat in which we cross the sea of dualism to reach the shore of oneness. And linga is what gives bhakti the needed focus and direction. Again, linga is not the end but a means to go beyond, to reach nirakara, the formless, Supreme Reality. Without bhakti and linga worship, I believe, it'll be like going round and round in a desert land, reaching nowhere.'

Breaking into a smile, caressing his beard, Allama said, 'When the whole universe is the temple of Shiva and the sky the linga, where is the need for yet another symbol, Chenna Basava?'

Several saranas, notably the senior saranas, who all adorned the front row in their shining orange robes, nodded their heads and smiled generous smiles, not because they were in agreement with Allama, but because Allama was not being snappy. Emboldened by Allama's counter challenge, Chenna Basava asked, 'Doesn't linga represent more simply and effectively what you are saying? Or, do you think all external forms are meaningless?'

'I didn't say meaningless. But, yes, quite unnecessary.'

'On the contrary, I think it's absolutely necessary,' argued Chenna Basava with great vehemence. 'Just as a ritual when performed with a sincere and pure mind is a stepping stone, a symbol is a springboard to that which is beyond. Just as through rituals you connect with the unknown, through form you connect with the formless. A pot is not without space, though you might say that that space is constricted and limited by the pot. But actually, it is a matter of realisation through devotion, discipline, rigour and experience. And with that realisation form becomes the formless. So I would argue and maintain that form is formlessness.'

'True-true...' chanted the saranas. 'Form is formlessness! How very correct and beautiful!

His fingers pecking at his beard, eyebrows raised in a frown, Allama remarked, 'Brilliant play of words!'

Marayya, a senior sarana, who resembled Allama in his long beard and long hair, stood up and asked, 'Prabhudeva, why do you deny the obvious? Why do you doubt the indisputable? A kite that plays about freely in the untrammelled air needs an anchor, doesn't it? Similarly, can a cartwheel move without solid ground under it? Likewise, can there be bhakti without linga? And without linga, can one come upon emptiness? O, Prabhudeva, why do you ridicule linga worship?'

'Don't be silly,' Allama snapped at the senior sarana. 'I'm not against linga worship. Did *I* ask you to stop worshipping the linga? What does it matter to me whether you worship the linga or a tree or some boulder? It is your life, your fate.'

Haralayya now stood up with folded hands. 'We want your blessings,' he said, bowing his head in respect. 'But you are not giving them. Why are you so indifferent, so unsympathetic to the ways of common people like us? You may not feel the need for symbols, but we do. Everyone is not like you.'

'I'm not here to fool people,' Allama exploded. Whether common or uncommon. I'm not asking anyone to do what I do, or to be like me, or follow me. In any case, you can't follow me, and you can't follow yourself either.'

As Haralayya sank back in his seat, a huge groan erupted from the gathering. Several saranas were now getting restless and even annoyed with Allama, because he was getting snappy and offensive again. Basava showed no reaction, but he looked pensive. And Siddarama, his hands folded over his chest, sat as if deaf, yet a thin smile playing on his lips.

'Prabhu, this is unfair,' Chenna Basava reacted angrily. He had gone red and had leapt to his feet. He had never been so frustrated and annoyed before. 'We know that before coming upon this supreme realisation and understanding, you too did go through rigorous sadhana. One time you too had a guru, worshipped the linga, and performed tapas. Why then do you deny the same to others? Every master in the past, as it has been the case with you as well, has gone through a process, a method, a path. It is natural, inescapable; I would even say absolutely necessary.'

'Shut up,' shouted Allama. 'You may have studied all the books in the world and performed all kinds of sadhana, but you are not free of anything. The more you argue the more hollow you sound. Don't be a fool. Learning to be quiet when required is the sign of a wise man.' Then standing up tall in his long, flowing beard, he continued in a strident voice.

'There is no guru, no linga, no jangama, no padodaka, no prasada, no vibhuti, no rudraksha and no mantra. No method, no process whatsoever. If your elders, whom you call masters, either of the past or of the present have talked of a process, a method, a path, then, they were and are all misguided fools. Just forget about them. Don't ever mention them to me again. They are all no match to the little toe of my left foot.'

Chenna Basava stood speechless, as if he had been struck by lightening, his face turning ashen. The saranas couldn't believe their ears. Allama had not only silenced their invincible Chenna Basava, but had even called him a fool. The only person in the assembly who appeared to be indifferent to Allama chiding Chenna Basava was Ganadeva, who continued to write with a long, pointed pen.

Presently, Allama turned his gaze upon Basava, and now calm, said, 'Basava, I think you should speak now.'

Getting up from his seat in his long gown, Basava took a step forward, folded his palms in greeting, and then he turned and slightly bent his head in a show of respect to Allama. Then resuming his straight posture, he spoke.

'Why all this long debate about form and formless? Does a lover need proof of love before he begins to love?' Surveying the saranas, he paused significantly and then continued, 'Tell me, can prana exist without a body? Can the face see itself without a mirror? Of what significance or worth is inward knowing, if that can't express itself in the outer world?' He paused again to huge murmurs of approval from the saranas, and then he continued, now in a voice charged with emotion. 'Linga is that body, Linga is that mirror, Linga is that inner vision assuming a form in the external world.'

'Yes, true, true, very true...' chanted the saranas. 'Why all this long debate, O, Kudalasangamadeva!'

'You may sing passionately profound lines,' Basava continued, 'you may listen to the great puranas and you may speak eloquently the philosophy of Vedanta, but, with no bhakti in your heart, it'll be like washing a toddy-pot from outside.'

Chenna Basava, back in his seat, was beaming triumphantly. Siddarama could not help smiling. Even Basava was challenging Allama now. But then the debate could not have gone in any other way, mused Siddarama. And he knew that Allama was playing one of his wily games to the hilt, and to perfection. Siddarama now turned and saw Allama laughing in his beard quietly, and his heart stopped when Allama went up on his feet again.

Now no more harsh, but in a voice that was loud yet grave, Allama said:

> Born to earth as rock,
> shaped by a sculptor,
> turned into an idol in guru's hand,
> as what do I worship, this bastard,
> born of these three?

There was a huge groan of extreme shock and strong disapproval. Siddarama saw several saranas put their hands over their ears and wince. Ganadeva lifted his head and looked at Allama, doubting if he had heard him correctly. It was most blasphemous, and Allama, his eyes now burning red, looked the very personification of blasphemy!

Chenna Basava was in rage, but he had no courage to stand up to Allama. A great, almost palpable silence pervaded the hall. It was terrible, frightening, like facing a tidal wave moments before death. It was fear and it tasted bitter! Only Nage, sitting in the back row, looked extremely amused, and on the dais, now, Basava smiled, adjusted his turban and stood up again. His palms folded together, the smile still playing on his lips, he chanted:

> Lord, your sacred feet
> cover the earth and sky,
> extend to the underworld and beyond.
> The crown of your head
> touches the boundaries of the boundless space.
> O, Kudalasangamadeva,
> both visible and invisible,
> mysterious is your form,
> now come alive as Linga in my palm.

And as Basava held his ishtalinga in his left palm raised at the eye level, the saranas leapt to their feet and erupted into chanting: 'Om namah-shivaya-Om namahshivaya...'

Staring at the saranas going frenzy with joy, Allama gently rose again from the Throne of Void. Slowly, huffily yet dreading the worst, the saranas resumed their seats and held their breath.

Allama thundered:

> He is not the three-eyed one
> reigning over the three worlds;
> not the one in rags, wearing
> garlands of skulls and roaming the forests.
> He is not Isvara, nor Maheshvara;
> Guheshvara Linga is beyond thought.

Basava bowed his head thrice to Allama. Then he replied:

> Without anubhaava bhakti is empty;
> without anubhaava linga is unattainable;

> *without anubhaava one understands nothing.*
> *When such is the truth, why call*
> *anubhaava an invention of thought,*
> *O, Prabhudeva?*

The saranas now sat on the edge of their seats, spellbound by the exchange between Allama and Basava. Siddarama, too, all too involved in the terrific exchange, gazed upon Allama, astonished at the way he drew the generally quiet and gentle Basava into the debate.

Allama, now smiling, now caressing his beard, said:

> *If there is no desire,*
> *there is no imagination;*
> *if there is no imagination,*
> *there is no thinking;*
> *if there is no thinking,*
> *there is no Guheshvara;*
> *if there is no Guheshvara,*
> *there is no truth,*
> *no void, either.*

Quickly, Basava countered Allama thus:

> *You exist*
> *like light hidden in the horizon,*
> *like a frame in a picture,*
> *like meaning in a word,*
> *O Kudalasangamadeva!*

Allama smiled, and fired his last salvo:

> *Escaping the claws of the cat*
> *waiting for it in the loft, the rat*
> *hid itself in its eye.*
> *With the separation gone,*
> *nobody ever saw Lord Guhesvara.*

The saranas were stunned by the mind-boggling imageries. What was Allama saying? What do the cat and rat represent here? And rat hiding in cat's eyes? What does it mean? It seemed so simple, yet so profoundly complex and confounding. But Basava smiled. He knew there was no stopping Allama, there was no stopping the roar of silence. He put his palms together and closed his eyes for a while in deep thought; then, opening his eyes, raising his voice, chanted:

> *I saw a lion come,*
> *devour another*
> *and itself die.*
> *I saw inwardness*
> *without an interior,*
> *outwardness without refuge.*
> *I saw in a field*
> *flowers without petals, and*
> *beheld a magnificent form*
> *take shape,*
> *and the whole world*
> *become a wonder.*
> *O Allama Prabhu,*
> *salutations to you.*

Immediately, taking the cue from their master and in tune with him, the saranas rose to their feet and chanted: 'Allama Prabhu, namo-namo ...'

Frowning, Allama too stood up and slowly raised his hand, gesturing at the saranas to quiet down. As the adulating chant died down, for the first time, Allama put his hands together in salutation, and said, 'Blessed is the land to have a son such as Basava, blessed are the people to have a brother in Basava, and blessed are the saranas to have a guru in Anna Basava. Anna Basava, salutations to you.'

❖❖❖

The same evening, as the night crept on Kalyana like a thief, and the lamps set on pillars lighted the streets and crossings of the town, when Allama and Siddarama joined the saranas for a dasoha, Nage went with Bahurupi to his house for dinner. Bahurupi's wife, Paru, slim and fair, with large eyes and a round, cheerful face, was all smiles.

'Brother,' she asked Nage in mock anger, 'what took you so long to visit your sister?'

'Your jealous husband wouldn't invite me.' Nage replied teasingly. Bahurupi growled dismissively. Paru giggled.

'But you know something,' she said to Nage, 'your friend wants to renounce the family and become a sanyasi!'

Bahurupi hissed and frowned. Nage laughed, and when the children were brought before him, he affectionately ruffled the hair of the five-year old son, gently pinched the plump cheek of the little baby girl, and asked, 'What's her name?'

'He wants to call her Shivangi,' said Paru, throwing a mischievous grin at her husband.

After dinner, over which Nage narrated hilarious anecdotes from their travelling days, with Bahurupi scowling and laughing alternately, with Paru giggling continuously and over-feeding the two men, the two friends went out to have a quiet chat by the Tripuranthaka Lake. At that hour, there was hardly a soul there, and, with a clear moon looking over, the lake slept undisturbed. Seeing that Bahurupi was hesitant to speak, Nage opened the subject, asking, 'Is everything all right now?'

As if he had been waiting for an opening, Bahurupi said, 'I don't know. But I'm learning to take things as they come. You know, I have realized one thing and that is, we are always, always either expecting, demanding change on our own terms, or, resenting, resisting change that has already come about, because it goes against our expectation.'

'So, what do you think must be done?' asked Nage, looking amused.

'Both are wrong. Of course, it is easier said than done. But I'm trying, trying to see through the games we play.'

'Ah! Games we play!'

'Aren't we all playing games?'

'Playing games according to our expectations, rules, eh?'

'That is the source of our conflict and much violence, no? Rules, rules and more rules. All of us have a set of rules that we think should be good for everyone. But it doesn't work and the game is spoiled.'

'You think Allama was playing games this morning?'

'I'm not too sure,' Bahurupi reacted slowly, thoughtfully. 'I thought Allama is the only one who is truly beyond all these games. But now, I suspect that he too plays games and gets angry when we don't abide by his rules.'

Nage shook his head. 'No,' he said vehemently. 'I think Allama Prabhu is critical of all rules. He is against all games played according to some fixed rules. And that is his game, if you still want to call what he does a game.'

'But doesn't his game have any rules at all?' asked Bahurupi doubtfully.

'I think I got it,' cried Nage excitedly, like one who had suddenly come upon some profound secret. 'There are only games, no rules. But the moment we want to impose rules, the problems begin.'

'Is it ever possible?' asked Bahurupi, screwing up his face and shaking his head. 'A game implies rules. There can be no game without rules. It is simply not possible.'

'Precisely,' agreed Nage, getting rhapsodic as he continued, 'there cannot be a game without rules, and yet, we never play a game strictly as per the rules, and therein lies the great irony, the eternal conflict and the root of sorrow.'

'But if there are no permanent rules, what then?'

'O yes, there cannot be permanent rules. There are no permanent rules. You said it,' shouted Nage, making Bahurupi wonder if he had at any time in the past seen his friend in such a state of excitement. Indeed, Nage was euphoric, as if it was a moment of great illumination. And now he continued, as one in a trance, 'There are no permanent rules because there is nothing permanent, including your relationship with your wife and children, including Allama's teaching!'

'But does Allama really have a teaching?'

'Teaching against all teaching, against all rules which can never be followed by anyone, much less by the teacher himself.'

Bahurupi stared at Nage, at his long hair, sharp nose and big eyes, as if he was seeing and hearing him for the first time. He chuckled, and asked, 'Nage, my friend, you really have started speaking like Allama. Tell me, by any chance, are you his long-lost younger brother, or should I ask, his long-lost younger sister?'

'I'm neither, but I'm Allama's enemy number one,' he said, with a wicked glint in his eyes.

Mahadevi's Trial

It was an event the like of which was unheard-of in the annals of their history. Women abandoned their household chores, men their gossiping, children their games, old people their bedstead and soldiers their posts, and they all rushed out to the street to behold the awesomely beautiful spectacle.

About twenty women, ranging between the ages of eighteen and forty-five, walked up the street, their heads held high and smiling bright like the morning sun. Among the lot were Gowravva, the one who had nursed Mahadevi while she was unwell; Somavva, one-time prostitute and a recent friend of both Nage and Bahurupi; young Ashwini, who had started composing vachanas when she was hardly twelve; Gangamma, who had become a widow at the age of eight; Guddamma, a tribal woman; and Gangadevi, an unmarried blind woman. Her body covered by her long, curly tresses, Mahadevi walked in the front, and it was a sight even for the gods to watch.

While some ogled unabashedly at the women and some cackled and shrieked and howled, many were transfixed with wonder. At times waving their hands at the crowd, otherwise their palms folded in greeting, these strange and wonderful women strode up the main street, their steps reverberating through Kalyana.

As more and more people poured out onto the street, the soldiers swung into action to control the crowd. Women who, quite excited, wanted to touch Mahadevi, touch her feet and seek her blessing, had to be physically pushed back. Young women tore freshly worn fragrant flowers from their hair and tossed them on the path of these weird and marvellous visitors. Drums, pipes and horns were brought out and the sky burst with music. Many saranas, their hearts swelling with emotions they had not experienced before, chanted: '*Om namah-shivaya, Om namah-shivaya...*' Soon, all along the street, people began to repeat the mantra and the collective chanting reached a deafening crescendo. Suddenly, it was like a festival, like celebrating the victorious return of the emperor from battle.

This emotional upsurge and wild greeting was something totally surprising and unexpected. But Mahadevi was only too keen to reach Anubhava Mantapa as fast as she could and meet with Basava and Allama. Her hands folded in salutation, looking neither to the right nor left, Mahadevi hastened her pace towards the Hall of Experience. His joined palms held up in greeting and respect, his back slightly bent, a beaming Kinari Bommanna stood at the gate to welcome Mahadevi and her companions. Returning the greeting, her heart pounding, Mahadevi stepped into the Hall of Experience.

The reception there, in direct contrast to what she had received out on the streets, was a deafening silence. But, evidently, they all had been waiting for her arrival. All heads turned in her direction as she entered the aisle. She saw on the dais five men sitting on chairs and gazing at her. In the middle, in what looked like a massive, magnificent throne, perched a bearded figure in a long ochre robe. She knew the bearded one was none other than Allama Prabhu. The one in turban, sitting to his left, his face wreathed in a warm smile, was Anna Basava. To Allama's right sat the legendary Guru Siddarama. The young man to the right of Basava was surely the scholarly Chenna Basava. But she had no idea of the man sitting next to Siddarama. However, all their eyes stared at her as if in unbelieving wonder. Still, no one spoke. The silence was unnerving, intimidating. Mahadevi smiled, intoned the name of her Lord, put her palms together, and bowed.

'What is all this fanfare about?' the voice of Allama suddenly boomed over the hall. 'Why have you come here instead of going to your husband's house?'

The women behind Mahadevi were stunned by Allama's sudden, baffling offensive. So this is it, thought Mahadevi. From the day she had left Uduthadi months ago, she had only been looking forward to meeting Basava. A couple of days ago, while passing through a village, she had learnt that Allama too was now camping at Kalyana, and she had thought that she was truly blessed to be able to meet the two masters at the same place. And here she was now, so close to living her dream, but greeted with ominous silence, stern looks and harsh queries, in complete contrast to the way people had greeted her on the streets of Kalyana. It was as if the Hall of Experience had sucked into its belly the maddening cries of joy and hooting and rendered the moment empty and hollow, like a shell without the nut.

Mahadevi braced herself to answer the question. It was Mahadevi's moment of truth.

'Prabhu,' she said, 'you ask a strange question. Still, if I have to answer it, I have come here as the daughter-in-law of this house.'

'Daughter-in-law? Ha-ha-ha...' laughed Allama. 'But who is this husband of yours?' Though most of the saranas sat tight-lipped, puzzling over the cruel yet intriguing ways of Allama, a few could not help sniggering.

'Of what use have I of husbands who die and decay?' Mahadevi answered, unflustered. 'Throw them into the kitchen fires. The One with no bond nor fear, no clan nor land, no birth nor death, no place nor form, my Lord Chennamalikarjuna, He is my husband.'

'Ah, you speak well!' said Allama. 'The whole world can see that you are quite young, and beautiful, too. Umm, just a little girl, and you speak of Chennamalikarjuna and Kadali in your vachanas! Tell me, what do you know of Kadali? What is your experience?'

'Prabhu,' Chenna Basava cried out. Distressed and angry, he rose in defence of Mahadevi. 'You know pretty well that age has nothing to do with anubhaava. Age or growing old does not automatically bestow wisdom on anyone. If it does, then, all our elders, all those whose hair grew long and grey doing tapas, even those with wobbly legs and shaking heads, who stammer silly nonsense, should be called wise.'

'Well said, Chenna Basava,' exclaimed Siddarama from his seat. 'We can gauge the age of timber, but can one measure the age of *arivu*?'

'Let her answer,' said Allama.

'Prabhu,' Mahadevi answered, 'are you really troubled by my young age and body? And don't you know what Kadali is? Kadali is this body, this mind and these senses. Kadali is this dense world and impenetrable forest. I have penetrated this forest and triumphed over this world, and in every pebble and every leaf I have seen the face of my Lord Chennamalikarjuna. I am nothing but His now, lodged in His lotus heart.'

Sounds of great approbation and appreciation burst forth from the gathering of the saranas. Greatly impressed by Mahadevi's answer, Basava smiled gladly and was about to rise and welcome Mahadevi formally amidst them, but on seeing Allama raise his finger, he slid back. When Allama opened his mouth, nobody spoke. Seated on the Throne of Void, he was the leader, the king in command.

'Don't you think I'm impressed,' Allama said. 'You have still not answered my question. The whole world knows that you were married to King Kaushika, that you betrayed his trust in you and ran away. You think our saranas here will be impressed by a woman like you?'

This was too much, thought many saranas. How could he be so cruel? On what grounds was he assuming that they were all critical of Mahadevi when none of them had spoken a word about her? And he was not even offering Mahadevi a seat!

It was like a trial through fire. How strange, Mahadevi thought, even in this gathering of great spiritual masters, the onus of proving her innocence, her integrity, was entirely on her. Gowravva, who was standing right behind Mahadevi and was quite upset by Allama's rude interrogation, whispered, 'Mahadevi, you don't have to answer this question.'

But Mahadevi answered.

'I did not betray Kaushika. In fact, he betrayed my trust in him. He broke his promise. While I was into my prayers, breaking his word given to me, he came in and pulled at my sari. And I walked out. You may think it was a small mistake on the part of Kaushika. It was not. We had agreed that if he were to break his word of honour, I would go free. So I walked out free. That is my story and that is the truth.'

She paused, wondering if there was anything more she had to say to clear the doubts. She looked around and saw a thousand pairs of eyes fixed on her. Let it be, she thought, let everything come out and be cleansed.

'Men and women blush when a cloth covering their shame comes loose,' She said. 'But when the entire world is the eye of the Lord, overlooking everything, what can you cover and conceal?' She paused for breath, and continued, 'Prabhu, there is nothing that I can call my own. Absolutely nothing, not even this body. Everything is His. And when everything is His, what is there to hide? When this body, cleansed of all impurities, has become one with the Lord, what does it matter how it looks?'

'Clever, very clever,' gurgled Allama. 'You say you are nothing and speak as if you have gone beyond the consciousness of your body. Why then have you covered yourself? If there is nothing to hide, why then do you hide your body behind those tresses of yours?'

This was quite unwarranted and too indecent, murmured even the senior saranas. But Siddarama, unafraid, expressed his disapproval. 'Prabhu,' he said, 'is it necessary to hammer what is already pure gold to test its purity?'

'It is necessary and you'll soon know why,' said Allama snappily and then turned his attention on Mahadevi again.

'Prabhu,' Mahadevi said, 'I cover myself for the sake of the world, lest people see in my body what is not there. And it is to protect others and not myself, nor to hide anything. Does that trouble you, Prabhu? Are you still not satisfied with my answers?'

'No, I'm not convinced,' bellowed Allama, feigning anger. 'You speak as if you don't have a body, as if you don't exist. It is like a dead body declaring itself dead, like curdled milk claiming sweetness. Is it possible?'

'But, Prabhudeva,' Mahadevi replied, unruffled. 'When one wakes from a dream in which one has died and talks about it, isn't it like a dead one speaking of one's own death? When curdled milk is boiled, isn't there sweetness in it? Should this matter be argued further, Prabhu? But then I have nothing more to say.' And she bowed her head as if to say she was finished and fell silent.

Allama was suddenly up on his feet, now smiling and clapping his hands like a little boy who has won a bet.

'There are no more questions to be asked,' he declared. 'You have solved the unsolvable, answered the unanswerable.' He paused, it seemed to give the saranas a moment to breathe freely and then, raising both his hands in a gesture of greeting and respect, he shouted, 'But why are you standing there. You have to come and sit here, on this Sunya Simhasana. This place is meant for you. You may be young in years, but in your maturity and vision, you are our elder sister, our Akka.'

'Akka, Akka, Akka Mahadevi...' Cries of joy burst forth on the hall, like a sudden rain pattering down from the heavens. Along with others on the dais, Basava leapt to his feet with folded hands, and in a voice brimmimg with emotion, said, 'Akka Mahadevi, we are blessed to have you amidst us today. Indeed, today is truly a blessed day!'

As the four men moved down the dais, Neela and Ganga rushed up the aisle and each taking Akka by their hands, led her to the front. Somavva, who had spotted her friends, Bahurupi and Nage in the back row, flung a big smile at them, as if to say, 'See, here I am.' Thrilled to see Somavva, waving his hand, Bahurupi pushed his way through the crowd towards her.

Quite amused by the emotional scenes all around him, Nage broke into laughter. A middle-aged sarana, who was standing by his side, gaping at the scene near the dais, disturbed by Nage's sudden loud laughter, asked, 'What are you laughing at?' As if tickled by the question, Nage convulsed with wild laughter and between his laughter, he shouted, 'My dear friend, what else can you do after witnessing this hilarious drama, this charade?'

'Charade? I don't get you,' said the man, frowning.

'Don't you understand? Ultimately it all comes down to this, doesn't it?' Calming down, Nage said, 'Who is interested in the truth, eh? It's just that we all want to feel everything is all right and safe. We all want to be friends, right? Look, look at the saranas greeting and hugging each other, as if they have found a great treasure hitherto unknown to humankind, as if they are now the custodians of truth. And look at those near the dais.'

'Yes, what about them?' asked the man, the frown turning into a scowl.

'Don't they all look comical,' said Nage, more as a statement than a question.

'I still don't understand,' said the man, now fuming with anger.

Pointing his finger at the ones near the dais, Nage continued stridently, 'All those men put together are no match for that little naked girl! And they want to test her character; they want her to explain herself to the world why she is the way she is. What impudence! What arrogance! And Allama plays along!'

'Friend,' the man warned, 'you are speaking nonsense.'

'That is what I'm saying,' shouted Nage over the increasing noise around him. 'All this is just pure nonsense. A well-staged charade! And you people think this is some great event that has to be recorded in golden letters? What a joke!' And he burst into yet another wicked laughter.

During the next two days, Akka Mahadevi attended the convention, but did not speak much. On the first day, saranas wanted her to share with them her newly composed vachanas. Looking ill at ease, Mahadevi said that she did not remember her vachanas.

'Mahadevi, you don't know how much we all have been waiting to hear your vachanas,' Neela said, thinking Mahadevi was feeling shy.

Mahadevi shook her head.

'Sister, forgive me. I don't remember any of them.'

It was then, Gowravva, who was seated behind them in the back row, now bending forward, asked, 'Mahadevi, shall I?'

During their ten-day journey to Kalyana, Akka had composed several vachanas; rather, they had been spontaneous utterances in different circumstances, some of which Somavva had promptly written down. Gowravva stood up, and, making her pranams to the saranas and the masters on the dais, recited:

> *Husband inside, lover outside,*
> *I can't manage them both.*
> *This world and that other,*
> *cannot manage them both.*
> *O Lord Chennamalikarjuna,*
> *I cannot hold in one hand*
> *both the round nut and the long bow.*

Then Gowravva recited another, which, in fact, had been Akka's poetic response to a question about her nakedness asked by young Ashwini.

> *You can confiscate money in hand;*
> *can you confiscate the body's glory?*
> *You can peel away every strip you wear,*
> *but can you peel the Nothing,*
> *the Nakedness that covers and veils?*
> *To the shameless girl wearing*
> *Lord Chennamalikarjuna's light of morning,*
> *where's the need for cover and jewel?*

There was a thunderous applause from the saranas. Bahurupi nodded his head vigorously and shouted out his appreciation.

'What are you getting so excited about?' Nage, who was sitting by his side, asked rather rudely. 'Tomorrow, if your wife were to say the same thing, would you allow her to go naked into the world? Just shut up and listen.'

'Come on, Nage,' Bahurupi said, laughing, 'there can be only one Akka Mahadevi. Only one in a million!'

Dipping his pen in the inkpot frequently, Ganadeva wrote briskly. He looked a picture of fierce concentration, repeating the words as he wrote them down. Just as he finished, he saw Somavva, blushing, stand up to recite the next one. He was all ears, and his mouth fell open.

> *Why do I need this dummy*
> *of a dying world?*
> *Illusion's chamberpot,*
> *hasty passions' whorehouse,*
> *this crackpot*
> *and leaky basement?*
> *Finger may squeeze the fig to feel it,*
> *yet not choose to eat it.*
> *Take me, flaws and all,*
> *O Lord Chennamalikarjuna.*

Trembling with emotions, Somavva repeated the last two lines *Take me, flaws and all, O Lord Chennamalikarjuna,* several times. Her involvement was so complete that she felt as if every line of it was written with her own blood. *Take me, flaws and all, O Nirlajjeshwara,* she chanted silently to her Shiva, the Lord without Shame, and burst into tears. Except for Mahadevi and the other women with whom she had come, and then Bahurupi and Nage who had met her before, no one else among the saranas knew she had been at one time a prostitute. Still, the fact that she could stand there as an equal among the illustrious devotees and spiritual masters and recite a vachana was indeed an overwhelming experience for Somavva.

A heavy, rather poignant silence descended upon the gathering. Gowravva, who knew the probable cause of her tears, held Somavva's shoulder in an affectionate gesture and whispered, 'Control yourself, Somavva.'

'Why are you crying?' Allama shouted from the dais. 'You should be jumping with joy and dancing!'

Allama's remark forced Somavva to hold back her tears. The next moment she forgot all about her dismal past when she saw Akka Mahadevi herself stand up with folded hands. Several eyes grew wide and the saranas held their breath as Akka now chanted in a voice they could not believe belonged to her.

> *Till you know it is lust's body,*
> *site of rage and ambush of greed,*
> *house of passion, fence of pride*
> *and mask of envy;*
> *till you know and lose this knowing,*
> *you've no way of knowing*
> *our Lord Chennamalikarjuna.*

The next one hour, it was as if a river of vachanas had been let loose into the Hall of Experience. Much inspired by the recitation of Akka's vachanas, the other saranas, mostly women, started to recite their compositions one after another. The recitations brought alive the saranas like nothing else did. Basava looked supremely happy, nodding his head now and again, and smiling approvingly. Allama, now crouched on the Throne of Void, looked a little bored. Only Ganadeva did not have a moment's rest.

To Kadali

'I don't know. I have never asked myself these questions and therefore I have no way of answering them,' Mahadevi said. It was the second day, she looked ill and out of sorts, and when she couldn't help not responding to the saranas who pestered her with many questions, she spoke as one from a trance. To most of the questions asked of her, she said, 'I don't understand the question, so how can I answer it?'

At one point, when Chenna Basava himself requested her to at least share some of her experiences, she amazed everyone with her blunt reply. 'I do not think I can speak of my experiences. Not because they are either too painful or personal or too sacred to be shared with others, but because I still do not know what to think of them. And even if I try and talk of them, that'll be of no use to you and in no way help you in your quest. I think each one should simply tread one's own path and not bother too much about what others are doing. I have not followed anyone; rather, I have followed only the voice of my Lord Chennamalikarjuna.'

'But,' one of the saranas insisted, 'I think that the struggles and the sadhana you have gone through may throw light on some of the critical issues confronting us.'

'I don't think so. On the contrary, it might even mislead you,' said Akka.

'Speak to us about bhakti,' pleaded another sarana.

'I cannot speak of bhakti,' replied Akka plainly.

'What is your way, Mahadevi,' asked Neela.

'Lord Chennamalikarjuna is my way.'

'What or who is Chennamalikarjuna?' asked Chenna Basava, keen on getting Akka to speak.

Akka did not answer. There was no answer. Since there was no answer, it was as if the question exploded in her consciousness and the body gave way. If Neela had not reached out and caught her from behind in time, she would have collapsed on the floor. Quickly, Neela and Ganga carried her out of the Hall of Experience to a guest room and tried to revive her with salts held under her nose, and when it had no effect, by spattering cold water on her head and cheeks. Akka did not move. Allama and Basava came in only to see Ganga in tears and Neela desperately still trying to revive Mahadevi. Her breathing was slowing down and the body was turning cold and stiff.

'Shouldn't we get a vaidya?' asked Neela, her face wracked by fearful anxiety.

'No, she has gone into samadhi,' said Basava, as one who knew too well such happenings.

'This is death,' uttered Allama, as if talking to himself, gazing fixedly at the body crouched on the mat, like a foetus. 'This is death,' he repeated gravely.

'She'll come back,' said Basava, more as a question than a statement.

'If she's destined to come back, she will,' muttered Allama, and, turning to Neela, he said, 'Don't do anything. Don't even touch her. Just keep a watch.' And then he turned and walked out of the room.

Hours later, just as the sun went down and lamps were lit in every household and Allama entered the room, Mahadevi opened her eyes.

'Get up and drink something,' said Allama, looking into her eyes that seemed lost in some other world.

Neela gave her milk in a silver cup. Taking the cup in

her hand, Mahadevi stared at the content, as if in wonder. And then she asked, 'What is this?'

'It is only milk,' said Neela as to a child. 'Drink it. You haven't eaten anything in the last ten hours.'

Allama smiled.

It took Mahadevi another three days to get back her memory and recognize people and things around her. But even during these days, she would now and then slip into a trance and then come back, her face glowing, but with a faraway look in her eyes. She hardly spoke, she only smiled whenever Neela tried to draw her into a conversation. Her body covered with ash-like substance, with vacant eyes, she squatted on the mat most of the time, looking like a strange animal in a state of hibernation.

On the fourth day, Allama sat by her and asked, 'So, what do you want to do now?'

'I don't know,' said Mahadevi, staring back at Allama, as if trying to recall who he was. 'I don't know,' she repeated slowly and fell silent again. Then, after what seemed a long time, she asked, 'Prabhu, what is this?'

'You tell me,' said Allama.

'There is only wonder, endless wonder. Everything, every piece of article, even a speck of dust is suffused with light, filled with infinite wonder. Nothing is what it seems.'

'Nothing is what it seems,' agreed Allama.

'Is this the end?

'It is only the beginning,' replied Allama, smiling knowingly. 'And you'll know what to do. But you can't stay here.'

'Kadali,' uttered Mahadevi suddenly. 'I have to go to Kadali.'

❖ ❖ ❖

Mahadevi's decision to leave Kalyana surprised and saddened Basava. Why did she come here then, only to meet them all briefly and leave? Or, was she destined to come to Kalyana to undergo that strange, mysterious experience and then proceed to Kadali? She had not talked about her experience to anyone, other than Allama; not even to Neela, who had day and night taken care of her like a mother would a child. Basava thought he knew and yet he was not too sure.

'Prabhu,' he asked Allama, 'is there something I have failed to understand?'

'Staying here will not do her any good,' Allama said, 'nor will it do any good to Kalyana.'

This was no answer; it only deepened the mystery. 'I don't know if it'll do her any good,' Basava said, 'but her stay here will certainly be a great inspiration to all of us.'

'I really can't claim to know what is happening,' said Allama. 'But I suspect she is finished with travelling and meeting people. Kadali is where she'll live.'

Basava was familiar with stories of yogis living and performing tapas in the caves of Kadali. But they were all men. How would Mahadevi, who was so young and inexperienced, live in such a dense forest filled with wild animals and fraught with all kinds of danger? Even the Chunchuras, the tribal people who lived on the fringes of the forest, feared to go into the forest. Wouldn't it be suicidal of her to live alone inside such a forest?

'Prabhu,' Basava said, 'it is not safe for Mahadevi to go there alone. I don't know, probably she has reached the last stage. But why Kadali, why not stay here? She needs to be taken care of. You were a witness to what happened to her a few days ago.'

'Are you afraid she would be gobbled up by some wild animal?' Allama asked, 'If that is her fate, if that is the will of her Lord, who can prevent it?'

To Basava it was not a matter to be taken so lightly and philosophically. But he did not argue. He only said to Allama, 'When her body was turning stiff and cold, you said, "This is death." And you know she was completely helpless and vulnerable and had to be literally taken care of like a child.'

'Yes,' nodded Allama. 'It is only the beginning and there is no going back.'

'*Aikya*,' Basava pronounced the word as if it was too sacred even to utter it. 'Are you saying that Kadali is where she'll attain it?'

'She is dying to everything of the past.'

Basava was too preoccupied with his concern for Mahadevi's wellbeing to figure out whatever Allama meant. He seriously believed Mahadevi needed protection and it was his responsibility to ensure that.

'Shall I speak to Mahadevi?' he asked, 'Wiping the gathering sweat on his forehead.

'You are a compassionate guru.' Allama said, smiling. 'You are ever ready to understand the saranas and do what you can to help their situation. You even give in to their demands and feel most happy when you see them happy. But, tell me, when it comes to your own deep experience of things, what do you do? Will you go by the dictates of your heart or listen to the advice of someone however great or wise?'

'Prabhu, you know, I live by the dictates of our Kudalasangamadeva.'

'And Akka lives by the dictates of her Lord Chennamalikarjuna. Let her go. Your job is over. Now all that you can do is to make things easy for her to leave.'

But it was not easy for Basava, nor for the women who had accompanied Mahadevi to Kalyana, nor for Neela and Ganga and all those who had grown fond of her.

'We left everything and came with you because we wanted to be with you,' Somavva said, tears streaming down her cheeks, echoing the feelings of the women who had all come with Akka to Kalyana.

'How can you leave us now? What will we do without you?' Gowravva pleaded, 'Please, let me come with you.'

'It's not my husband but you who inspired me to write,' Ganga said, 'I have just started and already you are leaving.'

Haralayya's wife, Suguna, placed a pair of newly made sandals near Akka's feet and Haralayya said, 'This is a small gift from my wife and me. Please accept.'

'You are the elder sister I did not have,' Chenna Basava said, his palms folded in respect and affection.

Finally, studying her with kindly eyes, Basava said, 'Akka Mahadevi, you have become a significant part of our history, nay, our life. So long as there is a single soul in this world searching and seeking union with Godhead, you'll be remembered and revered. I pray that Kudalasangamadeva's protection and blessings will ever be with you.'

Akka Mahadevi only smiled as she had smiled to every other person. She looked rather embarrassed than emotional. She seemed in a hurry to leave. At last, when Allama spoke, she looked up in his eyes and smiled like a little timid girl.

'What are you waiting for?' Allama asked, in his usual gruff manner,

Mahadevi bowed her head and made her pranams to the saranas around.

'I have seen what I wanted to see,' she said, gravely and simply. 'I have learnt what I wanted to learn.' Then taking the name of Basava, Neela, Ganga, Siddarama and Chenna Basava, she said, 'You all have shared your precious wisdom and showered your love and affection on me. I'm grateful. I feel blessed. But now I have to go and meet my Lord

Chennamalikarjuna.' Then turning to Allama, she only said, 'Prabhu, I feel blessed to have met you. I'll go now with your blessing.'

As the sun came up the Lake Tripuranthaka, and a soft breeze swept across the land like a mother's caress, wearing the sandals Haralayya and his wife had presented her, but her naked body covered merely in her long tresses that looked like Shiva's magical locks, Akka Mahadevi turned her back to the crowd that seemed on the verge of breaking into tears.

Basava's Trial

Sovideva was a handsome young man in his early thirties. His mischievous grins gave one the impression of a man given to seeking the pleasures of life rather than one who could rule over a vast empire. But looks were deceptive, and Basava knew only too well that behind the amiable and cheery exterior lurked a tough and ambitious brute. And he knew how in the last two years, Sovideva had been pestering Bijjala to make him the yuvaraja. So it did not come as a surprise to Basava when Bijjala announced his decision to make his son the prince regent.

'I'm sure he will be as efficient, considerate and kind as you always have been,' said Basava to Bijjala, and then he smiled warmly at Sovideva, as if to say that he was not being sarcastic in his remark.

'Yes, yes, he'll be a greater King than his father,' Bijjala gushed; then fixing his eyes on Basava, he asked, 'But, Basavanna, we are quite upset with you. For the last three weeks you have not cared to come and see us. May I know what kept you so busy that you forgot all about us?'

Basava blushed at the accusatory tone in Bijjala's voice. Bijjala had never spoken so bluntly and complainingly before. It seemed to be the sign of changes to come.

'If it is Shiva's wish...' thought Basava to himself and talked of Allama Prabhu's and Akka Mahadevi's visit, then admitted that he simply couldn't find time to come and see the king and apologised for the lapse.

Sovideva, who was seated next to the king and was keenly listening to Basava and grinning darkly, remarked,

'But you are our minister in charge of the treasury!'

Ignoring Sovideva, Basava said to Bijjala, 'But, Your Majesty, you know that I never failed to attend to my work at the treasury and I did send you periodic reports.'

'The figures don't tally...' Sovideva started to say, but Bijjala, with a wave of his hand, stopped him from speaking further. Then turning to Basava, he asked, 'Basavanna, how is Neela? Even she seems to have forgotten us!'

Where the Dikshits, Pandits, Damodaras and Mancharasas had failed with Bijjala, they had succeeded with Sovideva. They did not have to try too hard to turn Sovideva against Basava. Unlike his father he was never in admiration of Basava. And, as if in reaction to his father's affection and respect towards Basava—which he found to be a sign of fear and weakness—he had developed a deep dislike for Basava. Far from being in awe of Basava's great reputation, his social concerns and radical spirituality, he saw in him a potential danger to the kingly order. That morning, after the summons had been sent to Basava, he insisted on his right as the heir apparent to be present in the meeting. But Bijjala did not want the son to be involved in the dispute.

'If we don't put these saranas in their place, they would soon become a danger to us,' Sovideva argued. 'You already have given them too much freedom and see what that has resulted in. They think they are beyond the ambit of even the King's rule. This cannot be allowed. There is such a thing as tradition and such a thing as the law of the land. It is high time they are taught a lesson.'

Bijjala was quite disappointed. Sovideva lacked the discretion and tact required of a prince regent.

'Son,' he said, 'these saranas are not outsiders, they are our own people. It would be foolish to do anything that would turn them against us. They are in large numbers and growing stronger by the day, remember that.'

'What if the merchants and priests turn against us? What about the Jains, Shaivites, and Vaishnavites? They are larger in number and stronger, aren't they? In fact, all these groups are already very unhappy with the way you have been partial to Basavanna and his treacherous activities. Doesn't that concern you?'

'Son, don't go by what others say.' Bijjala knew Sovideva had been talking to Mancharasa and Damodara and that he was quite influenced by them. 'You should learn to keep these rival groups off from each other. We can't afford to allow an open fight between them. We can't afford to be seen siding with one particular community.'

'That's what you keep saying, father, but in reality, you are closer and more sympathetic to Basava than to others, at least that is what the other groups think of you.'

'Do you want to become a King presiding over a civil war?'

'Remove Basavanna from office,' insisted Sovideva. 'That at least would soothe the tempers of the upper-castes.'

'But Basavanna is a Brahmin by birth, you know,' said Bijjala.

'And that is why he is all the more dangerous,' said Sovideva, grinning. 'Never trust a Brahmin who has gone against his own community.'

'Why would I need a king's money?' Basava raged. 'I can't stand these ignorant fools who don't respect our Lord and are contemptuous of our saranas.'

Neela and Ganga and Boatman Chowdayya had never seen Basava in such rage before. But why did he have to suffer this humiliation? Why didn't he quit his post? On several occasions in the past, Neela had pleaded with him to stop working for the king. 'As it is you don't have enough time to do your own work; why do you have to burden yourself with this extra responsibility?'

'What are you trying to prove?' Ganga asked in her quiet, firm way. 'That you can manage both the worlds of the saranas and the king, that you can both be a master and a servant? Or, are you afraid of losing your power?'

Basava walked out without answering her.

Chowdayya had, years ago, advised Basava against leaving his post at the treasury and going back to Kappadisangama, but watching his master in agony now, he said, 'Kick this ministership, Basava. You don't need to serve under a king who is no worshipper of our Lord.'

Earlier, at the first sign of controversy, a few of the senior saranas had advised him to leave the court, and his critics had jeered at him, saying, 'Look at this self-proclaimed Shiva-bhakta serving a bhavi…' Basava had said, 'If going into a chandala's house, I do the lowest service well, sitting below the throne of a worldling like Bijjala, I serve the state sincerely; my only concern is to serve our Lord. But if I worry for my belly's sake, for my goods, wife and children, let my head pay for it.'

But now the situation had changed and changed too drastically, forcing Basava to rethink continuing in his job at the court. Bijjala was no more the powerful, shrewd yet liberal king that he had been all these years. Basava remembered with gratitude Bijjala's unequivocal support to him in his work during the early days. Bijjala had always looked upon him and treated him with respect and affection, though at times, he did make fun of and laugh at what he called Basava's 'too much of goodness'.

Six months ago, when the gang of Brahmin pandits and priests and pontiffs and the powerful business class had made allegations of corruption and sedition against Basava and had demanded his removal from office, Bijjala himself never made any accusation against him. Just before his leaving the palace that day, Bijjala himself had walked up to the door and said, rather apologetically, 'Basavanna, let me assure you that I do not believe in all these allegations made against you by these people. As a King I have to give them a hearing, you know that. And I have to at least appear to make these enquiries. But I know there is no substance in what they are saying against you. It is a clear case of gross misunderstanding and suspicion. But you should help me here, for you too have a responsibility in solving this crisis. Do not do anything too drastic and radical so as to upset the social order. You must know that as the King I cannot go against the ancient order and that I'm bound by the Dharmashastra.'

Basava had said, 'Should the inhuman and unjust discrimination against the lower castes and women continue? How can anyone justify these absurd beliefs and evil practices in the name of religion and God?'

'I know, I know,' Bijjala agreed, nodding his head rather impatiently. 'But you should help them see the truth, and you should ask your saranas not to be too hasty and aggressive. It takes time to change these age-old practices. We should have patience.'

'Tell me, Your Majesty, how can I ask the bhaktas to continue to bow their heads and bend their backs double to these people who have no hearts. Saranas are not my servants and they are no slaves to anybody.'

'But they listen to you; you are their Guru.'

'I'm no Guru,' Basava answered snappily. 'I'm as much a seeker as they are. They listen only to the voice of the Lord.'

Bijjala had lost his temper. It seemed to him that Basava was not trying to appreciate his efforts to prevent the controversy from turning into a major crisis. He said, rather harshly, 'Basavanna, I don't need to remind you that you are my minister and as a responsible minister your first duty is towards the King.'

'Your Majesty, as your minister I perform my duties sincerely; but if you find me wrong, you just have to tell me and I'll leave. But, with all humility, I must tell you that my first duty is towards God.'

'Leave then,' Bijjala almost shouted, turning red in the face. 'Leave and go back to your bhaktas and your God.'

The very next day, Bijjala had sent word for Basava and had apologised and begged him not to leave. 'I cannot find another Bhandari like you. You are a good man, a man of God, and I know you have nothing but the welfare and happiness of people in mind.'

All that had changed now. That morning, in the presence of his son, Bijjala remained silent most of the time during the enquiry. At first, of course, he had tried to stop Sovideva and conduct the enquiry himself in his own soft yet shrewd way. But Sovideva did not give him a chance. And Bijjala withdrew into a shell, though, it seemed, reluctantly. He could not have shouted and scolded the prince regent in front of others. But then, who knows, thought Basava, it was quite possible that Bijjala himself had planned it all in advance and let his son do the dirty job.

And the allegations, made against Basava six months earliera, surfaced again. Sovideva did not give a moment to Basava, either to explain or counter these allegations. He needled Basava with a barrage of questions and insidious remarks. Hostile but clever, he never said he believed in the accusations and yet never gave the impression that Basava could be innocent either. Often he harped upon the 'reports' he had received from various quarters and he put his own views in the mouths of other people. 'According to one of these reports,' he said, 'money has been siphoned off from the treasury to build shelters and feed the saranas. In the last ten days, about eight thousand saranas were sheltered and fed at twenty-six dasoha centres. Where did the money come from for all these activities? And who were these saranas anyway? Reports say that a considerable number of them are thieves, thugs and anti-social elements, who exploit, bully and beat up innocent people. Did you know that recently a businessman was found murdered in his warehouse? A gang of five saranas were suspected to have committed the crime. But soldiers did not arrest these criminals. You know why? Because these soldiers were bought off. A sizeable number of soldiers too have become saranas. What do you say to this, Basavanna? And you know, the question often asked about you is: Is Basavanna really doing social service? Is he engaged in building a religious order or an army in the name of bhakti and God? Why do his followers call him Basavaraja and Basaveshvara, if they did not look upon him as their King, as God?'

Before Basava could even begin to counter the allegations, Sovideva, smiling broadly and shaking his head, ended the enquiry.

'Most revered and loved Basavanna, take your time, discuss it with your people and we'll meet again.' And he stood up, signalling that the meeting was over.

And Bijjala did not speak a word.

That evening, when Basava himself presented the whole case to Allama, Allama only said, 'But, Basava, why do you have to put yourself in such a vulnerable position?'

Basava was in a quandary. For one thing it was not all that easy for Basava to walk out on the king who had been so kind and supportive to his cause. For another, he was not too sure if by his relinquishing the post, his enemies would not persist with their malicious campaign against him. On the contrary, he could become a soft target, and it would be much easier for them to turn the king against him.

Basava approached Allama yet again for his advice.

'Basava,' Allama said, sensing his dilemma and anguish, 'your life at the king's court is over and done with. Don't look back.'

Allama had never been so direct and categorical in his staements before and that helped Basava make his decision without hesitation and with a clear conscience. His resignation coincided with Sovideva's investiture as the yuvaraja. He did not attend the ceremony.

Basava knew his days at Kalyana were numbered. Neela wanted to go and speak to Bijjala, but Basava stopped her, chanting his mantra: 'Whatever happens happens by the will of Shiva. Mysterious are His ways.'

When the news spread among the saranas, they could not decide whether to feel happy or sad over his leaving the court. But when they heard that Bijjala had handed over the reins of power to his son, Sovideva, they were seized with a sense of foreboding that their lives wouldn't be the same again. And then their anguish deepened when Allama expressed his intention to leave Kalyana. Why at this hour of crisis? He only laughed and said, 'Every moment is a moment of crisis.'

Neela and Ganga begged him to stay at least for the wedding of Sheelavantha and Kalavathi, for which the preparation had already begun. The nineteen-year-old, dark, tall and handsome Sheelavantha was the son of Haralayya. And the sixteen-year-old, fair-skinned, round-faced, pretty Kalavathi was the second daughter of Madhuvarasa. Madhuvarasa was the son of the renowned Rig Vedic scholar and notoriously fierce Brahmin, Pandit Sharma, and was himself a Sanskrit Pandit, but now a fervent follower of Basava and author of several inspiring vachanas.

On learning about Allama's decision to leave Kalyana, both Haralayya and Madhuvarasa approached Allama and beseeched him to stay for the wedding and bless their children. 'All they need is to be left alone to live their own lives,' said Allama, rather mischievously. But when both Kalavathi and Sheelavantha came and sought his blessings, staring at them as if he was seeing the most beautiful thing on earth, and smiling affectionately, he said, 'Be happy.'

Overcome with emotion, when Kalavathi broke into tears, Allama asked teasingly, 'Why these tears now? Wait till the wedding is over.'

'Prabhu, I'm scared,' sobbed Kalavathi.

'Scared of this fellow?' asked Allama, pointing at Sheelavantha.

'No, no,' cried Kalavathi, breaking into little giggles. Then wiping the tears with the pallu of her sari, she said, 'I'm scared of our future, Prabhu. You think we'll be allowed to live in peace?'

'Why should anyone allow you to live in peace?' asked Allama, frowning. 'You have made a decision and you should have the courage to live the way you want to. Anyway, don't you worry. You'll be all right.'

'So there'll be no trouble and we'll be safe?' Sheelavantha asked, desperate to hear yet again Allama's words of reassurance.

'What do you expect? Isn't marriage trouble?' Allama laughed, and both Kalavathi and Sheelavantha laughed too, feeling as if a great weight had been lifted off their chest.

But Basava remained a worried man. Three days earlier, when Siddarama wished to leave for Sonnallige, he had been relieved to know that Allama wouldn't be joining him. But now, Allama's sudden decision to leave added to his distress. He knew Allama could not be tied down to a place. He was like a wild bird in constant flight, like a river with a million legs forever on the move. It had been indeed their good fortune that he had stayed at Kalyana for at least these many days. But wouldn't he stay for a few more days? Wouldn't he? Basava badly needed his support and counsel at a time when he thought he had reached the most critical phase of his life. He had never felt so low and depressed before. It was not so much a despair he felt as a great sorrow, like a moonless night that crept into and pervaded his being.

'Prabhu, I'm at a loss,' he confided to Allama. 'I feel this great urge to leave everything and go back to Kappadisangama. I think my work here is over, but I'm not sure.'

'Do you have a choice?' asked Allama.

Basava sighed, and said, 'Prabhu, you know, I have no life I can call my own. I'm not the doer of anything; it is all the doing of Lord Kudalasangama. If anything, I'm only a channel, an excuse for His incomprehensible ways.'

'So what is the worry?'

'I don't know,' said Basava, feeling uneasy, 'I have this premonition of something bad happening and it makes me sad.'

'"Things standing shall fall, but the moving ever shall stay." Your words, Basava.'

'Yes, I know,' said Basava, nodding wistfully. Then in sudden doubt and great anxiety, he asked, 'Prabhu, are you saying it is all over?'

'Nothing gets over completely, Basava, you know that,' answered Allama gravely. 'Something is always left behind, some residue, and there'll be yet another beginning. But it is not in our hands.'

Nodding his head pensively, Basava asked, 'Is that why you are leaving?'

'Do I have a choice?' asked Allama, smiling through his beard.

'Prabhu,' Basava said, his eyes growing moist, his heart quivering with a feeling he did not want to name, 'I don't know. All that I have said and done are mere bubbles on the surface of the sea of this samsara. I see them burst and I see there is nothing. I really don't know, Allama Prabhu. Mysterious are the ways of the Lord! I'm only a bhakta, bleeding, yearning to be one with Him.' Basava paused, wiping the tears off his eyes. He looked ready to die, to plunge into the infinite murmur of silence. Hesitantly, yet helplessly, he asked, 'Allama Prabhu, before you leave, won't you say something, give me some advice?'

Smiling as one amused by Basava's confession and request, Allama said, 'Basavanna, you must know that I have nothing more to add to whatever I have said so far. And you must know that whatever I have said so far has no relevance whatsoever at this moment. It is past, dead and gone. Nothing is permanent, including all that you have built with your tears and blood in the name of your Lord Kudalasangama. Just let things go.' Then, without speaking another word and without looking back, his long silver hair streaming on the breeze behind him, Allama Prabhu started to walk away from Basavanna, away from Kalyana.

Massacre in Kalyana

To the loud chanting and resounding drumbeats and boisterous music bellowing from several clarinets, the wedding of Sheelavantha and Kalavathi went off without any incident. The saranas had been well prepared to deal with protest or even violent intrusion by the upper castes. And even anticipating the possibility of soldiers descending on the marriage hall and stopping the ceremony, saranas had positioned themselves at strategic points to prevent the soldiers from getting in. All these arrangements had been done secretly, without the knowledge of Basava.

It was a marriage that would change history. It was a fearless and thunderous expression of their faith, and denunciation of the varnashrama dharma. The tradition viewed marriage between a Brahmin woman and an untouchable man the most sacrilegious of all possible inter-caste marriages. A son born out of such a couple was condemned to remain a *chandala*, an outcaste, *anamika*, the nameless, and unfit to live in society. Manu, the lawgiver, decreed that a chandala dare not even look at a Brahmin. He should not be allowed to live in any town or village. Alone he should roam, but only on the periphery of the civilized world, keeping only dogs and donkeys as his companions and clad in the garments of the dead.

It was not as if there had never been cases of Brahmin women having sexual relationship with shudra men or even ati-shudra men. But such cases were few and far between compared with Brahmin or upper-caste men entering sexual liaisons with shudra and ati-shudra women. However, never had there been a formal, open wedding of the kind the saranas performed between the Brahmin girl and the untouchable boy. It was tantamount to making a bonfire of the Dharmashastra which damned varna-sankara, the intermingling of castes through marriage, and punished most severely the perpetrators.

To the saranas, however, the tradition according to the shastras did not matter, or it mattered only to the extent that the decadent tradition had to be overcome. Also, there was a simple logic to this wedding that was lost upon the followers of chaturvarna, and the doubting saranas, who thought it was an extreme step. The day Haralayya and Madhuvarasa received diksha and wore lingas on their bodies, they had severed their links with the caste they had been born into. They were saranas, plain and simple, with no caste identity and therefore, no caste duties to be followed. So then, the wedding was seen not as a marriage between a Brahmin and an ati-shudra, one outside the caste hierarchy, but between two young Shiva saranas.

His back erect, upturned palms gently resting on his crossed legs, Basava sat immersed in meditation. A long time passed and he felt a disturbance somewhere outside of him. His eyes were closed and yet he could see, through an inner eye, as it were, some kind of pressure building up around him. He saw waves and waves of them circling, hovering over him and trying to penetrate his head. They were thoughts, each one with a density and colour and force of its own, waiting to find an opening to get in, like bees hovering over flower petals before plunging in. Sometimes in singles, sometimes together, hordes of them, these thoughts rushed at him, but only to be bounced off the stillness of his mind. There was something terribly aggressive about these thought waves, like red-hot iron, exuding intense heat.

Basava did not move, did not relent. '*Om namah-shivaya*,' he chanted and stilled his mind further: it was like trying to close an opening, a tiny aperture of his mind. It was a struggle, for the opening refused to close and the scorching waves danced about wildly without a pause.

Neela and Ganga remained at the door of the puja room. A lamp burned faintly in a corner. They could see only his back, erect, swathed in stillness. This was not something very peculiar. At least for an hour or two, sometimes for longer periods, Basava would sit in his puja room, performing puja or praying or meditating. But there was something different today. He had looked grave and edgy. Soon after coming home from the wedding celebration, without uttering a word, he had entered the puja room.

The two women squatted on the floor by the door and waited. Another hour passed and still there was no sign of Basava coming out of his meditation. Time passed slowly, like an ox-drawn cart with a low burning lamp ambling through a country path on a moonless night. And then after a long wait, when finally the first rays of the sun swept in through the dark haze and swelled up like an intense prayer, Basava opened his eyes and stood up. At the door, both Neela and Ganga, their backs against the wall, had dozed off. Her lips slightly parted, Neela looked as if frozen in the act of saying something. Cheeks stained wet with tears that had not yet fully dried, lips pressed into a pout, Ganga's face looked wracked by unutterable pain. Basava did not want to wake either of them, did not want to stand there and let his heart give way and his resolution break. *O Kudalasangamadeva,* he intoned to himself, stepped away from his wives and entered his chamber.

And then he felt it, like a knife piercing through his heart, and his body went numb, just as Haralayya and Madhuvarasa, not far away from Mahamane, breathed their last.

❖❖❖

Hours before, in the thick of the night, soldiers had swooped down on the houses of Haralayya and Madhuvarasa and had dragged them out. When the dark waters in Tripuranthaka Lake turned silver and in the nearby Shiva temple the bell boomed, and when Basava stepped out of his pillared house, his heart now hard as steel, mind straight as an arrow, all was over.

Their eyes gouged out, their bodies tied to the hind legs of the two royal elephants and dragged through thorny bushes and over rock-strewn field, skin encrusted with layers of coagulated blood and mud, both Haralayya and Madhuvarasa breathed their last, chanting the name of the Lord. By the time the news of their arrest spread like wild fire and the saranas rushed out of their houses and came running to the field, the two elephants were standing innocently still, while the soldiers were untying ropes from the dead bodies.

To the wild chanting of the name of the Lord, with tears burning their eyes, the saranas carried the mutilated bodies and placed them in front of the Hall of Experience. Faith demanded a sarana to protect and support another sarana, even at the cost of his life. What should they do now? This was nothing less than the most heinous crime committed against their faith, against two of their most respected and loved saranas. Should they avenge this most horrible killings? Defying Chenna Basava's appeal and warning, the raging rudras began a dance of death.

But where was Anna Basava? Whatever happened to him? 'Anna Basava... Basavanna...' the agitated crowd hollered in one voice. Neela came out and said, 'Kalyana has become empty of Basava. Basava, Basava, the word has become a meaningless sound swallowed up by terrible silence.'

Not far away, in his palace, when King Bijjala woke up to the terrible news, he cried out, 'O, I'm ruined. Basava, forgive me and forgive my son of this great sin.'

And much against Sovideva's warning and his minister's plea not to stir out, Bijjala decided to go to Mahamane and meet Basava. But his arrival at the Anubhava Mantapa only drove the saranas into a mad fury. The soldiers and his personal bodyguards could exercise no control over the surging, raging crowd of saranas. Jagadeva, a young sarana, composer of twenty-eight vachanas and known for his ascetic qualities and daring mind, rushed at the king with outstretched arms as if to embrace him, and before anyone could realize his deadly intention and react, he struck a knife into Bijjala's chest. As blood spurted out and drenched his royal attire, in great agony and with his consciousness ebbing away, mistaking the figure of Chenna Basava rushing towards him to be Basavanna, Bijjala screamed, 'O, treachery! Basavanna, how could you do this?' and collapsed into the arms of a bodyguard. Jagadeva roared with laughter and bellowed, 'This is your punishment, Bijjala, for killing our saranas.' And the next moment he laughed and spoke no more, as another guard's sword swished across his neck and severed his head from the body.

All hell broke loose. Sovideva unleashed his elite army on the miserable saranas of Kalyana. It was not a battle between two forces, but a massacre of the hapless yet courageous saranas. Groups of brave saranas who challenged the soldiers were cut down mercilessly. Thousands of saranas fled Kalyana. With the help of a few armed saranas, carrying the precious and sacred texts and his own records of the vachanas and discussions held at the Hall of Experience, Ganadeva managed to escape to Sonnallige. Neela, Ganga, Chenna Basava and some senior saranas too had no choice but to go into hiding.

Bahurupi and Nage had a narrow escape when they ran into a group of marauding soldiers. One of the soldiers, who, mercifully, happened to be Bahurupi's relative, recognised Bahurupi and let the two go unharmed. But Nage was not so lucky when they entered a narrow alley and chanced upon a group of vengeful, armed saranas. They recognised the storyteller, and the humorist, too; but, unlike the soldiers, they would not let Nage go free.

'He is my partner,' cried Bahurupi. 'He is Nage, Nageya Marithande, our famous humorist, don't you know?'

'Yes, kill him for his bad jokes,' roared a bearded sarana.

'What are you saying?' screamed Bahurupi. 'He is one of us. He is a Shiva sarana.'

'He is not a sarana,' barked another one. 'He is our enemy. He makes fun of our God and ridicules our faith. He deserves to be killed.'

'Don't be foolish,' shouted Bahurupi. 'You don't know him...' But when he saw two saranas approach Nage and Nage break into a wild laughter, he was seized with fear. He grabbed one of the saranas by hand and pleaded, 'Believe me, Anna Basava himself thinks highly of him and has even called him our voice of sanity, our balancing factor, our laughing sage...' and Bahurupi spoke no more and shut his eyes just as the bearded sarana swung his heavy club down on the head of Nage, who kept shaking with laughter.

Om

Bahurupi unwound his flame-red turban, pulled it around his neck, tied up the lose ends at the back and began a dance. It was a slow, rhythmic yet energetic dance he had learnt recently. He danced within an imaginary circle, sometimes flailing his hands in the air as in a trance. He danced as he sang and sang as he danced to the slow yet steady beat of the drum. The crowd sat enthralled by Bahurupi's strange dance and his new avatar in his long beard that seemed to sway meditatively along with him. But a few among the crowd soon got restless to hear Bahurupi's story of the evening.

The dance and songs were only a prelude to the story and meant to draw the attention of the people. Before long Bahurupi finished his dance, tied his turban back around his head and raised his folded palms at his eye-level.

'Om namah-shivaya...Om namah-shivaya...' Once the chanting trailed off like a summer shower, in his loud metallic voice, Bahurupi thundered:

'All stories, good and bad, come to an end, that is what many say. But that is not true. Stories are neither good nor bad and they don't come to an end, only storytellers do. Stories don't come to an end, but get abandoned, only to be picked up at some other time and at some other place. Nothing goes away, nothing ends; everything returns. The cycle of birth and death goes on and on and that is the meaning of impermanence. Nothing is permanent and yet everything exists. This is what we learn from our Allama.

'But our Nage is no more. Laughing, he vanished into thin air. We do not know where he went. Perhaps he returned to the abode of Shiva from where he had come. So it would be wrong to say that he is dead, for he lives on, lives on in your grins and smiles, giggles and guffaws; in the cool breeze among trees and thunder of the sky. And he lives in me through the stories, like waves in a sea. One day that too shall pass, but only to re-emerge in another time and place, in another form.'

Bahurupi paused for effect, but in that brief interval, someone in the crowd shouted, 'Come on, tell us the story?'

Bahurupi laughed a laugh that was reminiscent of Nage's throaty laughter, and then he bellowed:

'Everything is a story, a story within a story, always connected, never ending. You are a story, but you think your story is not good and interesting enough, so you come here to listen to someone else's story. But I tell you, another's story is also your story. They are all interconnected, and that is the reason why you want to hear other stories. And I'll tell you one more thing: everyone's story is good and interesting only if told honestly and in all its interconnectedness with other stories. In that sense there is only one story, the story of you and me, of this amusing yet complex world, of this awesome universe that keeps breaking out of all stories told from time immemorial.

'Look at me! My story should have ended a long time ago, but here I'm today, looking older than my age in my long greying beard. I was sick and bedridden for eighteen months. I survived. Maybe our Lord wanted me to stay alive and continue to tell stories. I'm all right now, I have got back my speech and energy to continue to disturb and trouble others. And you know something, my wife loves me, and my daughter has grown mischievous and started telling lies, such charming lies that even the good god would not doubt, which is really so reassuring, for I know that she is my daughter.'

This elicited a good measure of laughter from the crowd and then a few voices demanded, 'Yes, yes, tell us your story, tell us about Kalyana and what happened to our Anna Basava.'

Bahurupi suddenly pulled a stick—Nage's stick—out of nowhere and waved it in the air as if driving away invisible but menacing ghosts. Then he turned to the crowd and thundered:

'Listen and listen carefully. This is the story of Kalyana that doesn't exist as a geographical entity, but is felt to exist everywhere and indeed in every heart. This is the story of the child born of a barren woman, of the infant who died before its birth, of the snake who ate up the snake charmer, and of the rat that escaped the jaws of the cat and slipped into its eyes. This is the story of pralaya, the great destruction that killed off all the gods. And indeed, this is the story of maya that painted itself with the colours of the rainbow, and of the void that fell into the void and grew up in the void to sing without words, without sound, the song of life with no beginning and no end.'

Breathless, Bahurupi paused and inhaled deep the crisp air. And, as the crowd held its breath, he started again in his deep resounding voice:

'There is no Basava in Kalyana and Basava-Kalyana is no more. At the command of the new King Sovideva, the soldiers butchered about two thousand saranas and then, overcome with guilt at killing their own brothers and sisters, went home to cry in the arms of their mothers and wives. It is all over and yet it would be wrong to say that everything has ended.

'Chenna Basava has come back and has started his work quietly with a small group of saranas. His mother,

Nagakka, and Basava's wife, Neela, are with him, but most of the time confined to their puja rooms. We do not know where Ganga went or where she is; or, if she is alive at all. But we do know that Sheelavantha and Kalavathi are with Siddarama, at Sonnallige. Thay have a son and have named him Putt Basava.'

"What happened to Anna? Anna Basava namo-namo ..." The shouts and chanting struck the growing night like lightning.

'On the morning of the killing in the name of duty and sacrifice, Basavanna left Kalyana. Chowdayya took him in his boat across the Tripuranthaka Lake. Basava was a chaste young man when he came to Kalyana in Chowdayya's boat to work for the king as his finance minister. Chowdayya was his first friend, who, years ago, had stopped him from running away to Kappadisangama, and helped him plant and tend the *little plant* that eventually grew into a gigantic tree. It was a strange twist in this incredible tale for Chowdayya to be the one now helping Basava leave Kalyana and make his final escape.

'"Do you remember, Anna Chowdayya?" asked Basava, remembering the day Chowdayya had helped change the course of his life.

'Chowdayya was in his late sixties now, his hair had turned silver-white like the sun-streaked clouds in the sky, but his arms were strong enough to row the boat, though not as deftly as he used to in his younger days. He now gazed upon his old friend and Guru and was relieved to see no trace either of regret or pain in his face. He said, "I remember, Basava, and I wonder!"

'"Mysterious are the ways of our Lord!" chanted Basava.

'"Is it all over, Basava?"

'Basava let his hand down by the side of the boat, felt the cool water swirl around his fingers and felt himself as if cleansed of all doubts and questions. The sun had now come up the horizon, painting the lake silver-grey. Basava said, "We do not know, Anna Chowdayya; only He knows."

'Chowdayya smiled, and said, "You know, I ferried Allama across the lake. I asked him the same question."

'"What did he say?"

'He said, "Let go the question Chowdayya, and just row the boat."'

'And they spoke no more, the two old men. On reaching the bank, Basava stepped out of the boat, put his palms together and chanted, "*Namah-shivaya!*" Boatman Chowdayya returned the greeting: "*Om namah-shivaya!*"

'Bereft of his jewelled turban, clad in a simple dhoti and bare-footed, Basavanna walked for two days to Kappadisangama. It was forenoon when he reached the place and went straight to the matha. The young Guru, Shivaguna, was both surprised and overjoyed to see Basavanna and soon the bhaktas and several people from the village gathered in the Matha Square to have darshana of their Anna and seek his blessings. While the people squatted on the ground in the open square, wondering about his unexpected arrival amidst them, Basavanna sat on a raised platform and spoke his last words. He looked sad and angry and calm and collected alternately as he spoke in his deep, profound voice. He said:

'"Mysterious are the ways of our Kudalasangamadeva. We do not know. Sometimes in our ignorance and arrogance we think we know, but we really do not. Everything moves and exists according to His Will. All that we can do is to surrender ourselves, surrender our will totally and wholly to His Will. And that is Bhakti and that is what I have struggled to realize all these years, but I do not know if I have achieved it.

'"But enough of all that. Words however profound do not help much. Teachings, however noble, do not take us to the abode of our Lord. I know this only too well, if you believe me. And I know you believe in me too much and take my words too literally and seriously. That is not necessary. You have to believe in yourself, in the voice of the Lord who speaks through your heart.

"'I have left Kalyana. It is the Will of Kudalasangamadeva. I have no choice. For whatever it has been worth, my work there is over. It is all over and done with. My mission as decreed by the Lord is over and my journey comes to an end here and now.

"'There is no way but the way of bhakti. But, beware, bhakti is like a cobra in a pitcher! Will you risk your hand in the pitcher? If you do, you'll know that you are no more there and that your sorrow and the sorrows of the world are only illusions and that there is only one truth, one reality, one Absolute Infinite that has no name, no form."

There was a long pause; it seemed as if the world had suddenly come to a standstill, and then abruptly loud murmurs and grunts of impatience erupted from the crowd. Smiling, Bahurupi continued:

'Yes, I understand your doubts and disappointment. That day, Basavanna spoke of no path, no ritual, no astavarna and no sthalas—all of which he had rigorously practised and taught for thirty long years. He was finished with his work, his teaching, his life as a seeker of truth and God. He did not speak of Kalyana, of the killings of Haralayya and Madhuvarasa, of the assassination of King Bijjala and the violent riots that consumed the lives of thousands of saranas—all of which he probably knew by then. He did not speak of Allama Prabhu, Akka Mahadevi, Siddarama, or the Hall of Experience, either. All experiences had come to an end in him, or they were all mere memories, whether good or bad or profound, to be discarded as old clothes, and go naked to meet his Lord.

'Basavanna was a man of action, and a man of a million words, too, but also one who deeply loved the silent flow and murmurs of a moonlit river. He was like the lightning hidden in a dark cloud, like a treasure hidden in the earth, like silence within sound. He was the fire in water. Listen to this vachana he composed ten years ago:

> *Feet will dance, eyes will see,*
> *tongue will sing, and not find content.*
> *What else, what else shall I do?*
> *I worship with my hands,*
> *the heart is not content.*
> *What else shall I do?*
> *Listen, my Lord, it isn't enough.*
> *I have it in me to cleave thy belly*
> *and enter thee,*
> *O Kudalasangamadeva!*

Tears welled up in the eyes of many in the crowd; some even started to sob loudly. The night was long and Bahurupi had not yet finished.

'The twilight lay on the land like a melancholic song, like one of Basavanna's many vachanas composed with a bleeding heart. Basavanna stood up. He was sixty-two years old, frail but with his back straight like the will of Shiva. He folded his palms in touching humility and said that it was time to offer his prayers.

'Nobody followed him, for they wanted their master to be left alone to commune with his Lord in silence.

'As Basavanna stood in silent devotion at the confluence of the rivers, the last rays of the sun plunged into Kappadisangama and then there was only the moon hovering over a tree behind him, like a witness from ancient times. Palms folded in obeisance to the Lord without name or form, his mind growing still and tense like a mother's womb about to deliver, our Basavanna stepped into Kappadisangama and stood waist-deep in her flow, and then, as he took another step and yet another, a chill penetrated into his body and his mind went numb, dusky waters swirled and eddied around him in primordial intimacy, and soon, like a wave in the sea, like a breeze in the air, Anna became one with Lord Kudalasangama.'

It took sometime for the people to dry their tears, calm their hearts and become attentive again. A full moon stood over them, the same moon that had witnessed Basavanna plunge into the meeting place of the rivers to meet his Lord.

Suddenly, like thunder, Bahurupi's voice boomed over them again.

'You want to hear the full story. Then you better sit up straight and listen. Hard is the way of life, harder still the way of bhakti. Talking of bhakti, you may want to know whatever happened to our Akka Mahadevi.'

'Yes-yes, tell us about Akka, Akka Mahadevi...'

'Then listen, open your hearts and lend your ears. This is the story of stories from the beginning of time, the story that began the moment humans began to think and wonder at the mystery of life and yearned to penetrate the secret of existence.

'Sky-clad, her mind becoming empty like a summer sky, how Akka trudged the long route to Srishaila over twenty days, nobody knows, or only Lord Chennamalikarjuna knows. At Srishaila, she bathed in the sacred underground spring, offered her prayers to Jyothirlinga and rested the night in a nearby hut. A jangama, past his middle age, met her and talked to her about his many doubts and sought her advice.

He said, "Blessed Akka, I remain a seeker. I have wandered the world and met all kinds of people one could imagine. I have put myself through every sadhana one could possibly undertake. But all that has amounted to nothing.

I'm the same old youth I was thirty-five years ago before I became a seeker of truth, the same person troubled by doubts and desires, passion and boredom, lust and hatred for things and people. Deep inside I have not changed. I really do not know what this truth I'm after, what is this God who is supposed to be the answer to all our questions. Outwardly, I am a jangama, a revered bundle of flesh and bones with a name. Inwardly, I'm no different from all those I have met in all these long years of my spiritual search."

"That is the beginning, isn't it?" asked Akka.

"How can you say it is the beginning when I have come to the end of my life? Tell me, what is the secret? You know; you must know."

"I do not know," said Akka, smiling. "But why do you ask me? It is for you to find out."

"But I want to know what it is that you have found. Tell me," he pleaded.

'Akka Mahadevi said:

> *I do not say it is the Linga.*
> *I do not say it is oneness with the Linga.*
> *I do not say it is union,*
> *I do not say it is harmony.*
> *I do not say it has occured.*
> *I do not say it has not occured.*
> *I do not say it is I.*
> *I do not say it is You.*
> *I do not say anything,*
> *for there is nothing to say.*

Without a pause, Bahurupi continued:

'I met this jangama last month at Kalyana. And you know, on learning about the terrible killings, he only grinned like a deaf old man, but while talking about his meeting with Akka, he kept giggling like a silly boy. He looked happy, much more relaxed than what I had seen of him years ago; he looked like a drowning man who had at last found an empty boat in the middle of a sea.

'Coming back to the story, the next day morning, Akka left Srishaila and climbed the hills towards Kadali. We do not know how she managed to tread that dangerous path all by herself and when she entered the dense forest. Weeks later, the Chunchurus reported to have seen her living in one of the caves deep inside the forest. Only the daring Chunchurus go deep into that area to get medicinal herbs that grow on the banks of a silent stream.

'Isn't it very strange that we know so little about this little girl who left Uduthadi to meet and marry the one with no clan, no caste, no place; the one who knows no death, nor decay, nor form. O, how this little girl became our Akka and in Kadalivana, following the path all her own, how she attained that final union is something that can never be known.

'Friends, maybe there is no such thing as ultimate knowing, no final answers. There is only bayalu, Emptiness, the Void that has no beginning and no end, what Allama calls the void within void within void...'

'Allama-Allama-Allama...' the crowd began to chant.

And Bahurupi sang:

> *Whence this great tree,*
> *whence the koel bird?*
> *Whence and what kind of relationship?*
> *Gooseberry from the mountain,*
> *salt from the sea,*
> *whence and what kind of relationship?*
> *O, Lord of the caves,*
> *between you and I,*
> *whence and what kind of relationship?*

'Allama, Allama, Allama Prabhu…' roared the crowd again and demanded, 'Tell us about Allama.'

'What do you want to know?' Bahurupi asked, 'You want to know about the Prabhudeva who at one time sang of the mysterious relationship between the tree and the koel, the gooseberry and the mountain, the salt and the sea, and his own enigmatic relationship with Lord Guhesvara, or you want to know of the Allama who denied and rejected all relationships as mere illusions, including the one between the bhakta and God? You want to know the Allama who never spoke, never uttered a word, yet composed ten thousand vachanas? You want to know where this Allama went and what happened to him? No. You don't want to hear this story. Forget it. Go home and sleep the night, hoping there would be another day.'

'Allama, Allama…' the crowd roared again with rising anger.

'You are asking for a story that will explode your heads into a million flinders, the story that will burn and reduce you to a heap of ash,' Bahurupi thundered and suddenly he was not himself.

'Tell us,' demanded a few harsh voices, 'otherwise, we'll burn you to a heap of ash…'

'That's what my wife warns me of every time I leave home. She says "Be doubly careful of what you say. I don't want our children to become fatherless."'

Peals of laughter broke through the crowd. And, as if in tune with the mood, a strong gust of wind blew over them and the flares danced about, a thin and angry looking man now stood up in the glare of the dancing flare and yelled, 'Finish what you started.'

'There is no choice, is there?' laughed Bahurupi, and started on his last story that was really his last but not the end.

'Listen, and listen with all your mind and body. For here is the end that is no end but only a nameless, formless beginning. One day, rather, seven days after he left Kalyana, Allama, our Allama Prabhu, stopped by a cremation ground and wondered: what is it that draws me to this corner of the field.

'He walked in and, all of a sudden, he was confronted by a terrific spectre: in front of him stood the awesome gods of the universe, their lustrous bodies, clear and solid now, dim and hazy now, like shimmering heat waves in a desert land. Allama broke into a laughter.

'"What are you laughing at?" asked the gods in one voice.

'Allama took some time to cease laughing. "Powerful is thought, eh? And you are the stuff thought is made of. Anyway, why are you all here? Is there anything I can do for you?"

'"Why are you so angry with us?"

'"Why?" repeated Allama, smiling mischievously. "It is in the nature of fire to burn."

'"Fear us," screamed the gods.

'"Fire burns everything, including fear, including gods."

'The gods giggled, looking at each other. "Are you challenging us?"

'"No, but I reject you all. Now get off my path," shouted Allama.

'"Be warned. Know that you are only human and surrender," the gods commanded. "Surrender and you'll be bestowed with power over the world."

'"Ah! The charming circle of deception! But I'm done with you and your illusory powers and goals; now leave."

'"Ask. Just ask and the doors of heaven shall open and all your desires shall be fulfilled."

'Allama laughed his wicked, throaty laughter. He said, "You are the ultimate desire that must be burned to cinders."

'"That'll be the end of you," warned the gods.

'Allama's his eyes turned red with rage and fiery sparks streamed out of them.

'The gods now appeared to be truly terrified. And they appealed together: "If you are finished with us, so be it. We'll have nothing to do with you from now on. But why do you involve others in this personal battle of yours. People need us, without us, their lives will be empty."

'"You charm and deceive them. You are like a menu without the meal. You are the wielders of illusion that must be destroyed."

'"This is your last chance..."

'"The play is over, now out of my way," roared Allama. "You are the greatest and last obstacle I must cross." In swelling rage, Allama stared at the gods. Paralysed by the burning gaze of Allama, the gods stood helpless, unable to escape. Now a searing blaze leapt from Allama's eyes and the scorching, blinding, cascading mass of white light circled the gods in no time. Then the blaze yawned wide and spread the length and breadth of the earth and reached the heavens, sending sundry gods helter-skelter in panic. There was a growl, then a terrifying scream, and one did not know if it came from the throat of Allama or from the fire, or from the gods. The flame spread rapidly and soon it reduced to a flicker and there was a mountain of ash where the gods stood once.

'Stepping forward, Allama picked the still-burning ash in both his hands and smeared it all over his body. He looked human no more and he laughed, his teeth gleaming white, like the moon on a dark night. He laughed, his wild, feral, apocalyptic laughter, and started dancing Shiva tandava...'

As the drums came alive, with growing wonder the crowd watched Bahurupi break into a dance: his arms, rather his whole body moving without volition, it seemed, in tune with the primal rhythmic force. The people did not know what to make of it, but they all sensed, a strange, deep churning of energy within them, and felt that it was a sign of some great change to come and their lives wouldn't be the same again...

Afterword

Naturally the story-buster Allama has a huge and terrific presence in the narrative, also the one and only sky-clad Akka Mahadevi, about whom we actually know so little. We are not even sure how old she was when she left her husband, shed her clothes and walked 'breast-to-breast with the cosmos', through towns and villages to meet with Allama and Basava and then vanish into Kadali to seek union with her Lord Chennamalikarjuna.

Basava was an extra-ordinary religious and social reformer, but not a mystic of the order of Allama and Akka. Yet, saints like Basava are the agents of historical changes. The religious and social changes he set in motion were of great historical significance and—though, over the centuries, his followers converted the new revolutionary path into yet another powerful caste—his teachings continue to inspire radical critique of the caste system and divisive politics and offer a spirituality of bhakti as a way to self-realisation. Nowadays we may refer to Basava, Allama and Akka and their followers as Virashaivas, but they never called themselves by that name. It was only centuries later that scholars referred to them as Virashaivas and the name stuck, although there is hardly anything 'vira' or 'bold' or 'courageous' about the followers and the religious and social activities of the many Virashaiva (read Lingayat) mutts, monasteries, today.

It seemed only through the fictional mode one could capture the spirit of the age and get under the skin of these characters to narrate their story. So you could call this narrative a historical fiction. Although I have used the privilege of a writer to invent a few characters and situations to tell the story, most of the characters portrayed and events depicted are historically true.

Almost all the early writings on the vachanakaras, the ones who composed vachanas, poems, are predominantly hagiographical. Even with the vachanas one could not be sure if they were not tweaked by the later scribes to suit their needs or relate to the aspirations of the times. However, with all these misgivings, the vachanas are still the only dependable guide for a writer today to gain entry into the period and into the minds of the vachanakaras. And it must be said that the vachanas, especially that of Allama, have largely influenced and shaped the style of the narrative. Once I decided to tell the story through Nageya Marithande and Bahurupi Chowdayya (historically real characters but of whom we know almost next to nothing) the narrative inevitably took the tone of a folk tale, and then with the presence of Allama burning through the entire process of the writing, the story structured itself, as it were, in the form of his 'deconstructive' vachanas, which stun the mind into silence and give us a sense of *that* which cannot be put into words.

This enthralling anecdotal narrative wouldn't have been possible without the information about and insights into the lives and times of vachanakars offered by many authors in their works. In this regard, I am grateful to several authors, especially to the late Dr. D.R. Nagaraj, Dr. M. Chidananda Murthy, Dr. L. Basavaraju, S.C Nandimath, Thippeswamy, Basrur Subba Rao, and A.K. Ramanujan. I am also thankful to the Telugu novelist Rani Shivashankar Sharma, whose book 'The Last Brahmin' inspired in the making of the character Pandit Sharma, to the late I.M. Shivakumar who provided me with books I needed and for his suggestions, to N. Manu Chakravarthy, Chandrashekar Babu, Sashidhar Vishwamitra, Renu and C.K. Meena for their support and encouragement.

Glossary

Adharma: Decline of morality, or ethical standards.

Advaita: The philosophy of non-dualism, especially of Shankara.

Ahalya: Wife of Gautama whom Indra seduced.

Aham: Egoism.

Ahimsa: Non-violence.

Aikya Sthala: The stage of Union with Shiva in Virashaivism.

Aikya: Union [with Shiva, or Infinite Absolute Principle].

Akka: (Lit. Elder Sister) Term used to refer to Mahadevi.

Anna: (Lit. Brother) An endearing form used to address or refer to Basavanna.

Anubhaava: Spiritual experience; direct, unmediated experience of the Infinite Absolute.

Anubhava Mantapa: "The Hall of Experience;" a section of Mahamane, Basava's abode.

Arani: A piece of wood of the *Sami* tree used to kindle sacred fire.

Arivu: Awareness.

Ati-shudra: An untouchable.

Atma : Spirit, or that which pervades in all beings.

Avadhuta: A spiritually realized person, who is indifferent to social rules and customs, who seeks no disciples, and lives in the vivid awareness of the oneness of life.

Bagevadi: A town in Kalyana.

Bayalu: Emptiness, Open Space, similar to the notion of shunya.

Bhakta: Devotee of God.

Bhakti: Devotion to God.

Bhandari: Treasurer.

Bhavi: A worldly person, who is not a Virashaiva, or a Shiva bhakta.

Bindi: A mark worn on the forehead by women.

Brahma: The creator God.

Brahmachari: A bachelor, one who practices celibacy in search of truth.

Brahman: Ultimate Reality or Principle

Chakras: Centers of energy in the human body.

Chandala: An untouchable.

Chaturvarna: The four-caste system.

Chennamalikarjuna: Lit. "The Lord White as Jasmine." Mahadevi's favourite name for God (Shiva).

Chit-ananda: Consciousness-bliss.

Dasoha: Partaking in offerings of food.

Devi: The (Mother) Goddess who slew Mahishasura.

Dhoti: A traditional lower garment worn by men.

Diksha: Initiation.

Ganga: The River Ganges.

Garbha gudi: Sanctum sanctorum.

Gautama: Sage in Ramayana.

Gowri: Name of Parvati, consort of Shiva.

Guhesvara: The Lord of the Cave (part of the refrain in Allama's *vachanas*).

Gunas: The qualities or properties of the universe, as well as traits of human beings.

Holeya: An untouchable.

Indra: The king of heavens.

Ishtalinga: A favourite, personalized *linga* worshipped daily.

Isvara: God.

Jangama: A wandering monk.

Japa: Meditation consisting of repeating *mantras.*

Jnani: One who knows, or has realized the supreme truth.

Jyothirlinga: (Lit. The *linga* of light.) The *linga* in Srisaila.

Kailasa: Abode of Shiva.

Kalamukhas: Religious sect existing at the time of Basava.

Kalpa: An aeon or era.

Kama: Cupid. The god of sexual love.

Kamandala: A pitcher carried by spiritual mendicants to carry water.

Kapalikas: Spiritual sect whose members ate from human skulls.

Kayaka: (Lit. 'of the body') Manual labor as a spiritual practice.

Kshatriya: A person of the princely or soldier caste.

Kudalasangamadeva: The Lord of the Meeting of Rivers; refers to Shiva.

Linga: The (phallic) symbol worshipped in Shaivism (and Virashaivism) as Shiva.

Maheshvara: (Lit. 'The Great Lord'), Lord Shiva.

Mahishasura: [Lit. 'the Buffalo Demon'] A demon, according to mythology, killed by the Goddess Devi.

Mangalavada: Region where Bijjala ruled before he became the king of Kalyana.

Mantra: mystic formula, an incantation, used in meditation, *japa*.

Matha: Mutt. A monastery.

Maya: Illusion, fantasy, play.

Moksha: Liberation, release.

Narada: The heavenly minstrel.

Nirakara: the formless, Supreme Reality

Nirlajjeshwara: (Lit. 'The Unabashed Lord') The name used in the refrain of Somavva's vachanas. Refers to Shiva.

Padmasana: Lotus posture in Yoga.

Padodaka: the water to wash feet or water sanctified by the feet of the guru.

Pallu: The loose-end of a sari.

Parvati: Shiva's consort.

Pippala: The holy fig tree.

Prabhu: Lord.

Prabhudeva: A honorific term used to refer to Allama Prabhu.

Prakriti and *Purusha*: The female and male principles of the universe.

Pralaya: The dissolution of the universe.

Prana: Vital breath.

Prasada: Consecrated food given to devotees as God's grace; the remainder of the guru's dish.

Puja: Worship.

Puranas: Mythologies.

Rama: A human incarnation of Vishnu. The hero of the epic *Ramayana*.

Ramanatha: God referred to in the refrain of Dasimayya's poems.

Rishi: A sage.

Rudra: The ferocious form of Shiva.

Rudraksha: Rosary or sacred bead.

Sadhana: spiritual practice.

Sampradaya: Sacred tradition.

Samsara: Worldly existence, cycle of birth and death.

Sangama: The meeting place of rivers.

Sangameshwara: The Lord of the Meeting of Rivers (Shiva).

Sanyasi: A renunciate, a monk.

Saptarshis: The seven sages.

Sarana: A follower of Virashaivism; a devotee of Shiva.

Sat: Existence.

Satsang: Spiritual communion.

Shaivism: A sect of Hinduism.

Shastras: That which has been decreed; precepts, rules, compendium, treatise.

Shivapurana: One of the mythologies in the Shaivite tradition.

Shudra: A menial or low caste person.

Siddha: (Lit. 'He who has achieved') A spiritually realized person. Also a spiritual practitioner at a higher stage of realisation.

Stambha: A pillar (as in a temple).

sthalas, phases of the Virashaiva faith, six in number.

Sunya (also Sunyata): The Void.

Sunya Simhasana: The Throne of Void.

Taladhwaja: A king in a Puranic legend.

Tapas: Spiritual rigor.

Upanayana: The sacred thread ceremony of initiation.

Upaya: Skilful means.

Vachana: That which is said, or verses composed by saranas, often extemporaneous.

Vachanakara: An author of vachanas.

Vaidya: a physician.

Vaishnavism: A major sect of Hinduism, wroshippers of Lord Vishnu.

Valmiki (Maharshi): The author of *Ramayana*.

Varna: Colour, caste.

Veena: An Indian musical instrument of the lute family.

Vibhuti: Sacred ash made of dried wood or cow dung. Smeared across forehead and other parts of the body by spiritual seekers, or followers of Shaiva traditions.

Yoganidra: The slumber of yoga.

Yogini: a female yogi.

Yuvaraja: Prince-regent.